Church-planting Voices

Church-planting Voices

Michael D. Noel

CHRISTIAN PUBLICATIONS, INC.
CAMP HILL, PENNSYLVANIA

Christian Publications, Inc.
3825 Hartzdale Drive, Camp Hill, PA 17011
www.cpi-horizon.com

Faithful, biblical publishing since 1883

ISBN: 0-87509-801-0

*This book is dedicated
to the church planters of
The Christian and Missionary Alliance,
past and present.
Their obedience to His call
and passion for rescuing lost people
have resulted in
healthy Great Commission churches
that are extending the kingdom of God.*

Contents

Church-planting Testimonies

Conclusion

Acknowledgments

My thanks to The Christian and Missionary Alliance church planters who have shared their stories here to inspire others of us. Thanks, too, to the members of the National Church Planting Committee, who backed me fully in this book project. District church planting directors continue to share with me their insights in this fascinating work, and I am grateful to them.

My thanks to Dr. Gordon Meier for his research on Alliance church planting in the past (which appears in this book as "Voices from the Past"). And a special thank-you to my wife, Karen, who has worked tirelessly in support of this project. Finally, my thanks to Dr. K. Neill Foster, Executive Vice President/Publisher, and the staff at Christian Publications, Inc., for their encouragement and support in getting this book to press.

Michael D. Noel
February 1998

Church Planting—A Do-or-Die Emphasis

Why such an emphasis on church planting? Why not channel all this energy into other important concerns? "The answer goes far beyond our desire to double in size from 1978 to 1987," says Rev. Paul Radford, national director of extension. "By using some simple mathematics, everyone can readily see that if we don't plant churches, we won't survive as a denomination.

"For example, our annual reports reveal that every year we open new churches and affiliate existing ones. But we also close some churches and lose others who end their affiliation with us. If we had opened *no* churches since beginning our centennial advance in 1978, we would have fewer churches today than we had then. That implies fewer people and a smaller base for missionary giving.

"A study of the churches started from 1978 to 1984 confirms these findings and emphasizes the vitality of C&MA extension work; about 45 percent of centennial growth still comes from new and affiliated churches. They were responsible for about 20 percent of 1984 conversion growth. And they gave about 5 percent of the total 1984 Great Commission Fund.

"In one of the larger U.S. districts, for instance, only eight churches have been opened since the centennial advance began. But those congregations account for better than one-fourth of the total gain in that district's inclusive membership. I'm not surprised by how much of our growth comes from extension work, but it is low compared to what we might see in the future. We're still learning how to plant churches. When we start 200 to 300 churches every year the *bulk* of our growth will likely come from them.

"Church growth, of course, is more than theories, numbers, charts and statistical comparison. It is a matter of life and death: 'He who has the Son has life; he who does not have the Son of God does not have life' (1 John 5:12).

"So what our task amounts to is this: There are 141 million unchurched Americans—more people than the total population for most countries of the world. And we simply don't have enough existing churches to reach all these people. Church extension doesn't just happen; it takes prayer, planning and hard work. As we approach our second century, church planting *must* be a do-or-die emphasis."

—*Warren Bird,*
The Alliance Witness,
October 23, 1985

<table>
<tr><td>CHAPTER

1</td><td># Planting the Power</td></tr>
</table>

> "But you will receive power when the Holy Spirit comes on you; and you will be my witnesses in Jerusalem, and in all Judea and Samaria, and to the ends of the earth." (Acts 1:8)
>
> "I am not ashamed of the gospel, because it is the power of God for the salvation of everyone who believes: first for the Jew, then for the Gentile." (Romans 1:16)
>
> "For the message of the cross is foolishness to those who are perishing, but to us who are being saved it is the power of God." (1 Corinthians 1:18)

The gospel of Jesus Christ is God's provision of power for living. By the power of Christ's name, sinners are saved, the lost are found, the sick are healed, the downcast receive hope and the bound are set free. The hope of heaven ultimately depends on whether a person receives this power and becomes a disciple of Jesus Christ.

15

The local church, comprised of believers, is responsible to take the gospel and plant it in every community and people group. Motivated by the urgent need of people and the sufficiency of His power to meet that need, we demonstrate our nature as obedient, reproducing disciples of the Lord Jesus Christ by planting churches.

And yet, two full decades of "church growth" teaching in the American Church have brought only a negligible growth in numbers of professing Christians in the USA. Statistician and pollster George Barna reports that *not one county* in the U.S. has grown in its percentage of professing Christians over the last twenty years. The National Association of Evangelicals and others have predicted that in our generation we are witnessing the closing of 100,000 churches. While the American evangelical Church has been busy focusing on reaching the unreached peoples across the oceans, a foreboding event has taken place. In terms of unsaved people, we in the USA have become the third largest mission field in the world.

In the face of these realities, many denominations—including The Christian and Missionary Alliance—are doing some soul searching. The Alliance has long been known for its commitment to evangelism and aggressive church planting overseas. Now it is faced with the reality that *America* is a multi-cultural mission field. In America's urban centers, virtually all of the people groups of earth are represented, yet our efforts to plant churches among them are less than minimal for a "missionary church."

Within metropolitan areas are large, un-churched mini-cultures such as Generation Xers who are not resonating with established churches. Surely the day has arrived when we must re-evangelize the U.S. and gather the responsive into new churches that will reach out intentionally to these groups.

This objective can never be accomplished apart from an awakened Church that owns responsibility for the evangelization of its near-by neighbors. George Hunter comments:

> There is something tragically seductive about a denomination reaching a stage of development where the pins on the map show established churches all over the state. The denomination begins to think of outreach as "finished" and settle in for the nurture and care of Christians. These churches then experience net membership decline until they rediscover their perennial apostolic mission.[1]

This book is all about rediscovering that perennial apostolic mission of spreading the power of the gospel everywhere through church planting. The best plan for the re-evangelization of America is by aggressively reproducing healthy Great Commission churches. Such churches will evidence a healthy, balanced life that cares for the growth to maturity of its people while constantly seeking out the lost. A church that balances its building and equipping ministries with its commitment to obey the Great Commission will be serious about multiplying its ministry and sending out those God raises up with the apostle's call.

In the chapters that follow, we will review the New Testament pattern of church planting and then share the stories of eighteen new church plants—fresh evidence of an emerging church planting movement across the United States. We will conclude by looking at some of the blessings and challenges that can be expected by those who accept the challenge to reproduce a healthy Great Commission Church. May God speak to your heart!

Note

[1]George G. Hunter, *To Spread the Power* (Nashville, TN: Abingdon Press, 1987), p. 18.

Voices from the Past

Establishing New Churches

To reach lost men our Lord went from village to village proclaiming the good news of salvation. This was extension work in its purest form.

The crowds flocking to Jerusalem at feast time did not take the place of our Lord's going to them in their own villages. Neither can the strong voices of our large city churches replace the need of taking the gospel to outlying areas. Extension is more than bringing the sinner in; it is taking the gospel out. We dare not omit the first and we must also include the second.

It is always easier to wage a battle in home territory than it is to carry the battle into enemy territory. The work of extension is the establishment of spiritual beachheads in the strongholds of Satan. That accounts for the large number of casualties. Satan would persuade us to overlook the beachhead entirely or discourage us by reminding us of our disadvantage in such an assault. He would endeavor to destroy our landing party. If that fails, he seeks relentlessly to cut our supply lines.

As long as the ministry of extension remains a spiritual beachhead on Satan-dominated territory we can never expect the problems to disappear. But by God's grace I believe we can decrease our casualties and give reasonable assurance that as the problems appear they shall be overcome, and many self-supporting, soul-winning churches shall result.

—Rev. Alvin J. Moser,
The Alliance Witness,
July 30, 1958

CHAPTER	**Rooted in**
2	**Jesus**

Church planting is rooted in Jesus' own ministry and values. A quick review of the Gospels reveals that Jesus Himself laid the foundation for church planting.

The Mission of Jesus

The story of Jesus' encounter with the social outcast Zachaeus, recorded in Luke 19, gives us a glimpse of Jesus' sense of mission. While passing through the town of Jericho, Jesus confronts this man who "wanted to see who Jesus was" (19:3). Hindered by the crowd that pressed around Jesus, Zachaeus proved he was a true seeker by overcoming the obstacles that separated him from the Lord. You see, Zachaeus was "vertically challenged"—he couldn't see over the crowd! So he climbed up a tree in order to glimpse the Savior. (It is interesting to consider how many people seek Jesus from "up a tree" in their lives!)

Matching this remarkable effort on Zachaeus'

part was Jesus' responsiveness. He stopped beneath the tree, called Zachaeus by name and then invited Himself over for supper. While others avoided this "sinner," Jesus sought to befriend him. The text indicates that when shown this kind of acceptance, Zachaeus "came down at once and welcomed him gladly" (19:6). As the people muttered about Jesus going to be the guest of this well-known sinner, Jesus allowed His schedule to be "interrupted" by the need of a tax collector.

We can imagine the scene: Jesus first listens to Zachaeus tell his story and then offers him salvation through repentance and faith. Zachaeus rises to his feet to offer restitution to those of whom he has taken advantage. Jesus' response is one of affirmation. He exclaims, "This man, too, is a son of Abraham" (19:9), and thus welcomes Zachaeus into God's spiritual family.

Jesus' next words reveal His mission: "For the Son of Man came to seek and to save what was lost" (19:10). Lost people matter to God! Seeking out and saving lost people is "job one" for the Christ and all who would follow Him. When we seek, find and disciple the Zachaeuses of the world through church planting, we continue Jesus' mission.

The Passion of Jesus for the Lost

Jesus' passion to find the lost is illustrated in this remarkable series of parables. The opportunity to teach this value arises when the religious establishment sought to denounce Jesus: "This man welcomes sinners and eats with them" (15:2). Jesus tells three consecutive stories about lost entities: a lost sheep, a lost coin and a lost son.

Finding the lost sheep, said Jesus, is a higher priority than staying with the ninety-nine that were safe (15:4). The found coin becomes the source of great rejoicing among the woman and her friends. God's compassion and longsuffering are highlighted with the return of the prodigal son. The father never gave up on his delinquent son's return: "While he was still a long way off, his father saw him and was filled with compassion for him" (15:20). He saw his son in the distance because he was *looking* for him. When the prodigal reappears, his father is ready for him and throws a huge party. "For this son of mine was dead and is alive again; he was lost and is found" (15:24).

Contrast the father's attitude with that of the older son who harbored unforgiveness toward his brother and became angry when the prodigal was welcomed home. With seething resentment the older son protests, "All these years I've been slaving for you. . . . Yet you never gave me even a young goat so I could celebrate with my friends. But when this son of yours who has squandered your property with prostitutes comes home, you kill the fattened calf for him!" (15:29-30). Again the father emphasizes the importance of the son's return, "But we *had to* celebrate and be glad, because this *brother of yours* was dead and is alive again; he was lost and is found" (15:31-32, emphasis added).

Note the words used by the older brother to distance himself from his sibling when he says to his dad, "this son of yours." With disgust and contempt the older son insinuates that the prodigal has gotten what he deserves. Why celebrate with "sinners" like him! The older son seems perfectly content to have his younger brother lost and forgotten. But the father reminds the son that he too had a relationship with the prodigal and carefully chooses his words when he replies, "this brother of yours." The father's gentle rebuke to the older son is that his values are not in order. *There is no more important event than the restoration of that which was lost.* "There will be more rejoicing in heaven over one sinner who repents than over ninety-nine righteous persons who do not need to repent" (15:7).

The Confession of Jesus

One day Jesus decided to give His disciples a mid-term exam about His identity. He first asked them, "Who do people say the Son of Man is?" (Matthew 16:13).

After hearing their report, He asked the defining question, "But what about you? . . . Who do you say I am?" (16:15). Peter, speaking for the group, answered the question: "You are the Christ, the Son of the living God" (16:16).

Jesus accepted this answer and affirmed Peter for allowing the Father to give him this insight. Jesus went on to say, "On this rock"—the confession of Peter—"I will build my church, and the gates of Hades will not overcome it" (16:18).

Jesus promised to build *His* Church! The gates of the dark kingdom will be driven back by the power and authority resident in Christ's Church. As Christ builds His Church, He will systematically rescue the perishing from the clutches of the evil one. Those who engage in the ministry of church planting have simply made themselves available to a Lord who initiates and sustains the building of His Church among every people group worldwide.

The Progression of Jesus' Ministry

Notice Matthew's description of Jesus' ministry modus operandi:

> Jesus went through all the towns and villages, teaching in their synagogues, preaching the good news of the kingdom and healing every disease and sickness. When he saw the crowds, he had compassion on them, because they were harassed and helpless, like sheep without a shepherd. Then he said to his disciples, "The harvest

is plentiful but the workers are few. Ask the Lord of the harvest, therefore, to send out workers into his harvest field." (Matthew 9:35-38)

As He traveled from town to village, Jesus seemingly was motivated by the desire to get the message and the power to as many lost people as possible. He urged His followers to pray for workers to reap the harvest. Note also who the harvest belonged to. It was *His* harvest field. This was a regular pattern of Jesus as He moved from province to province. "After Jesus had finished instructing his twelve disciples, he went on from there to teach and preach in the towns of Galilee" (Matthew 11:1).

An interesting story is recorded at the end of Luke 4. After an extended period of powerful ministry, Jesus withdrew early in the morning to a solitary place, presumably to pray and commune with the Father. Soon the crowds discovered where He was and came to Him. In fact Scripture states that "they tried to keep him from leaving them" (4:42). They were so appreciative of Jesus' work among them that they wanted to keep Him to themselves.

Jesus' response is quick and decisive. " 'I *must* preach the good news of the kingdom of God *to the other towns also*, because *that is why I was sent.*' And he kept on preaching in the synagogues of Judea" (Luke 4:43-44, emphasis added). Jesus understood that he was under orders to take the gospel "to the other towns also." His mandate was to go from village to village, town to town and city to city. He set a pattern for us to follow in keeping an eye on the harvest just beyond the horizon. Throughout the ministry of Jesus, this concern to move the gospel to receptive and responsive people everywhere is obvious.

The Commission of Jesus

It was precisely this clear, habitual pattern that Jesus had set that made the words of the Great Commission so understandable to His disciples. In effect He is saying to them, "Just keep doing what you have seen me doing!"

"All authority in heaven and on earth has been given to me," He said. "Therefore go and make disciples of all nations, baptizing them in the name of the Father and of the Son and of the Holy Spirit, and teaching them to obey everything I have commanded you. And surely I am with you always, to the very end of the age" (Matthew 28:18-20).

This commission includes church planting. The command to "make disciples" is supported by three participles that indicate continuing action. He called the disciples to a ministry of reproducing themselves! As they regularly went out among the lost, they were to make converts from every nation (*ethne*—people group) and to disciple them by baptizing and teaching them. In this way indigenous churches were to be established where, ultimately, harvesters were raised up from the harvest.

Matthew 28:18-20 not only records Jesus' ministry assignment for His Church but also defines the *purpose* and *priorities* of the Church. Jesus commissioned the Church to "make disciples" from *all* ethnic groups. Jesus was concerned with the evangelization and discipleship of all people groups, whether they are the ethnic group downtown or the aborigines in Australia.

Jesus also promised an accompaniment of power to fulfill this responsibility. "You will receive power when the Holy Spirit comes on you; and you will be my witnesses in Jerusalem, and in all Judea and Samaria, and to the ends of the earth" (Acts 1:8).

He promises power for witness as the Holy Spirit endues the Church. Again we find a clear ministry assignment and sequence. The local church is to begin locally in its outreach. We might paraphrase Jesus' words: "I want you to begin here in Jerusalem and bear witness of me. Take your message to the surrounding towns throughout the region. Be sure you do not overlook Samaria. Though despised by some, they are not despised by God. As the way is opened by my Father, I want you to witness of me everywhere until the earth is full of the knowledge of the gospel." With broadening concentric circles we are commanded to reach out in witness until the "world is our parish."

In the ministry and values of Jesus we see the foundational roots that are the basis of church planting. The early Church recognized the pattern—and carried out the assignment. To this early Church pattern we turn our attention.

Voices from the Past

Six Daughters Are Not Enough

It was May, 1961. Rev. William E. Allen watched the scenery change from residences to steel mills to open farmland as he drove away from Mansfield, Ohio, and pondered the big decision he had been praying over for months. "Lord," he said, "You've brought so many people to our new building that we're already splitting at the seams. How can we adequately teach Your Word when Sunday school classes must meet in hallways and staircases? What should we do next?"

Pastor Allen wondered if he would find a solution when he got to Columbus, the site of that year's General Council. God's answer came through a missionary there. Rev. Paul S. Davis, on furlough from Thailand, told how a Thai C&MA church had successfully "daughtered" two churches in nearby villages.

The idea *sounded* great—but would it work in North America? Convinced that it could, Pastor Allen returned to Mansfield (Ohio) First Alliance Church and called a special meeting of the board. Soon after, as a result of that meeting, the congregation purchased five acres of land in a new subdivision named Westwood, seven miles away. Now, what would be the procedure for giving birth to a new church in that very location?

He placed two questions in the church bulletin, addressed to members living near Westwood: Would you be interested in joining a new congregation in Westwood? Or, if the church board asked you to go, would you be willing? In April, 1962, Mansfield First Alliance Church commissioned 98 people and its assistant pastor, James A. Davey, to form Westwood Alliance Church. By human calculations this sizable group—almost one-fourth of Mansfield First's regular attendance—would sap much vitality from the mother church.

Instead, the opposite occurred. For example, 12 of 22 choir members went to Westwood; but within two weeks Mansfield First's choir had swelled to 32! Both pastor and people quickly realized that no one can outgive God.

In only a few years Mansfield First was overcrowded again. The solution was to begin more churches—in Bucyrus (1969), Loudonville (1977), Butler (1980) and Shelby (1981). The first "granddaughter" church was born in Galion in 1984 through the nurturing of the Bucyrus congregation which sent 90 people to that work.

For many people in central Ohio, six "daughters" are not enough. Their family will be complete only after everyone possible, both here and overseas, has heard the good news of Jesus Christ.

—Warren Bird, *The Alliance Witness*, April 10, 1985

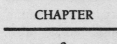

CHAPTER

3

Following the Pattern (Part 1)

Church planting was the means by which the early Church conserved the fruit of its evangelism. As the apostles spread out with their message of hope, their method was clearly to set up churches in every town they visited. Dr. Elmer Towns, author of the classic church planting primer *Getting a Church Started*, summarizes the first-century flow of the gospel this way:

> Beginning with the great dispersion of the Jerusalem believers recorded in Acts 8, the disciples successfully multiplied congregations and planted additional churches. In fact new congregations were planted in every pagan center of the then known world in less than four decades. . . . Based on the understanding of the eleven disciples and the success that resulted from their obedience, it is evident that planting local churches in every city throughout the world is God's plan.[1]

The *Church Planter's Manual* continues the idea:

> The Acts of the Apostles preserves the history of the spread of the gospel in the generation that followed Pentecost. This remarkable record is focused on church planting. The apostles considered no other option for expansion than to establish churches everywhere they preached, and evangelism was never divorced from church planting. No structures emerged for gathering the faithful other than the church.[2]

It seems that an intrinsic principle of church planting in the first century was that each new plant was in turn to assist in the continuing effort to plant new congregations. William Tinsley, Southern Baptist church starter, makes a strong statement about the centrality of church planting: "To remove the strategy of church planting from the New Testament would in effect remove all Scripture beyond the gospels. The disciples and apostles made church planting their strategy to penetrate first century society."[3]

The Early Church: Planting the Power

The Jerusalem church provides an example for us in the relationship of growth and church planting. Philip, a deacon from Jerusalem, fled to Samaria when the church was persecuted there. Prevented from returning home, he began preaching the gospel with encouraging results. When this news reached Jerusalem, Peter and John were dispatched immediately to assist the new work. What was lacking in ministry gifts was soon supplemented by the mother church.

Acts 11:19-30

Acts chapter 11 details the process of planting that began with the Jerusalem congregation and continued through its daughter, Antioch. Jerusalem believers, scattered by the persecution of Stephen, preached Christ in Antioch, far to the north of Palestine. People responded as a result, and a group of believers began to meet there. Luke explains the response of the church in Jerusalem to this exciting news.

> The Lord's hand was with them, and a great number of people believed and turned to the Lord.
> News of this reached the ears of the church at Jerusalem, and they sent Barnabas to Antioch. When he arrived and saw the evidence of the grace of God, he was glad and encouraged them all to remain true to the Lord with all their hearts. (Acts 11:21-23)

We can observe several principles of church planting at work from the account of what happened next.

First, we see that it is the natural instinct of the Spirit-led apostles to go with confidence in the search for new audiences for the message of salvation. There is a matter-of-factness in the way Luke tells the story. These early apostles were simply behaving in agreement with their nature.

Second, it is interesting that those who spread out from Jerusalem were significantly unnamed (11:19). They are called simply "those who had been scattered"—not apostles. With a firm faith in the providence of God over their circumstances, these ordinary believers went out in search of divine appointments. They believed that they had a mission to accomplish (Matthew 28:18-20) and that they would find receptive people somewhere. *The work they were about is the work of every believer.*

A third observation is that unreached people groups seemed to be the focal point of their search (Acts 11:19-20). Two distinct groups are named. The first targeted group was the Jewish population. The second targeted group was the Greek-speaking Hellenists. These distinct groups required different approaches and distinct strategies, which Paul models throughout the book of Acts.

"The Lord's hand was with them" (11:21), Luke writes, and He had promised to be with them always (Matthew 28:20). He had also promised them power to be His witnesses (Acts 1:8)—in other words, the Lord was present with His people in their work of witnessing. His presence brought an accompaniment of divine power and anointing, and the result of such anointing and sense of Christ's presence is that "a great number of people believed and turned to the Lord" (11:21).

Next we note that the established Jerusalem church gave supervision and nurture to the planted church (11:22-24). They sent Barnabas, a man of compassion and also evidently "the missionary gift," to investigate what the Lord was doing. He was apparently among them as they experienced a second wave of conversion (11:24). A movement of discipleship and reproduction was underway.

But who would disciple the new converts in the church plants? Barnabas responded to this need by recruiting Saul as a teacher. Barnabas and Saul shared responsibility for grounding this new congregation in the faith for one year. The mother church also sent other workers periodically to strengthen the daughter (11:27). This baby church became the first to be called "Christians" as they exalted their Savior and proclaimed the gospel (11:25-26).

The end result of this investment of resources and personnel was a maturing young church. It grew to the point that it began to minister back to the mother. Responding to Jerusalem's appeal for financial assistance, "the disciples, each according to his ability, decided to provide help for the brothers living in Judea. This they did, sending their gift to the elders by Barnabas and Saul" (11:29-30). What an encouragement and joy it must have been to the mother to see this partnership in ministry from its offspring! Its investment was reaping almost immediate dividends. Jesus Christ indeed blesses those who reproduce their ministry through church planting.

Acts 13:1-6

We pick up the story of this new church plant in Acts 13. The church planting and discipling soon brought forth gifted leadership (13:1). Whether those mentioned in 13:1 were among those residents of Antioch won to Christ and discipled or the leaders from Jerusalem that had been ministering to this daughter for some time (see Peter Wagner[4]) makes little difference. The fact is that the Antioch church plant had become sufficiently healthy to be in a position to move from "daughter church" to "parent church" in its own right.

In a profound demonstration of faith, the leaders of this young church opened themselves up to God's leading. While they were "worshiping the Lord and fasting," the Holy Spirit spoke clearly to the leadership team: "Set apart for me Barnabas and Saul for the work to which I have called them" (13:2). The time had come for Antioch to reproduce, and the Lord asked the church to give up the cream of its leadership team.

This understanding of God's call on them prompted another round of fasting and prayer (13:3). The leaders can be excused for wanting to make sure they had heard from the Lord correctly—they were being asked to send away probably the most beloved of the church leadership! This kind of leadership change must have been very unsettling for a young church. However, it did agree to give up its most gifted servants to "plant the power" among other unreached locales and cultures.

After holding a commissioning service they "placed their hands on them and sent them off" (13:3). The term translated "sent" here means literally, "they released them." What a wonderful picture this gives us of the attitude and faith of the Antioch church! They were willing to release or let go of their resources for the greater good of the kingdom.

Further study reveals that it was not only the Antioch church that sent them on but the Holy Spirit (13:4). With a clear understanding of their objective, with bold confidence that they would be successful because they were obeying God, they simply joined the Holy Spirit in what He was doing. Once again this church-planting team had a plan in mind: Reach a targeted people group and begin a pattern of ministry that will be repeated in town after town across Asia Minor and later Europe (13:4-6).

Acts 14:21-28

Wherever Paul and Barnabas evangelized, they left a church behind (14:21). They expanded new church plants to begin to evangelize and disciple and reproduce. As they made their way back toward Antioch, Paul and Barnabas stopped by each planted church to encourage, strengthen and exhort the new believers to "remain true to the faith" (14:22). They also appointed elders at this time to assure that discipleship and reproduction would continue (14:23).

It is noteworthy that these new church plants were built on basic spiritual disciplines like prayer and fasting (14:23). There is no mention here of Barnabas and Saul training the leaders in marketing techniques or fund-raising gimmicks. The future health of these new church plants was wholly dependent on the Lord and the churches' obedience to Him.

A Church-planting Pattern

In just two generations, the established church of Jerusalem had planted the church of Antioch, which in turn planted the churches of Cyprus and Asia Minor. The apostolic Church had established a clear pattern of planting churches that planted churches that planted churches. Jerusalem's initiative seems to have become the norm, and as the Word of God crossed over the ethnic barrier, even Gentile churches were planted. That small missionary force could never have penetrated the Roman Empire without the principle of church planting!

The epistles of Paul underscore the involvement of established congregations with newer works. Many times Paul refers to people in one congregation who are also associated with other churches in his letters. Timothy, Tychicus, Onesimus, Aquila and Priscilla, Aristarchus and Epaphroditus all apparently had a hand in the formation of more than one church. Furthermore, those churches with resources were expected to assist those who had less (2 Corinthians 8-9). In all probability this financial assistance was not only for the purpose of social relief for the poor but also for help in continuing the expansion of the gospel by initiating new church groups in all geographical areas.

The early Church's basic pattern seems to have been as follows:

1) New converts were gathered into churches;

2) Those assemblies soon generated new church plants. A central congregation would spin off "cell groups" and plant house churches all across a metropolitan area such as Thessalonica.

3) The congregation in that city then spread out to the surrounding province, evangelizing every village and city (1 Thessalonians 1:8).

The continued process of planting churches conserved the results of evangelism and expanded the capability of the Church to reach more people with the gospel. Each congregation created a new frontier for outreach.[5] The Savior's plan to evangelize the earth was launched!

Note

[1]Elmer Towns, *Getting a Church Started* (Lynchburg, VA: Church Growth Institute, 1985), p. 13.

[2]Keith M. Bailey, ed. *The Church Planter's Manual* (Camp Hill, PA: Christian Publications, 1981), p. 11.

[3]William C. Tinsley, *Upon This Rock* (Atlanta, GA: Southern Baptist Home Mission Board, 1985), p. 5.

[4]C. Peter Wagner, *Lighting the World* (Ventura, CA: Regal Books, 1995), pp. 147-148.

[5]*Churches Planting Churches Manual* (Nyack, NY: The C&MA Office of Church Growth, 1987), pp. 28-29.

Churches Are Born, Not Planted

The Lord Jesus Christ definitely declared, "I will build my church." This task He does not leave to the discretion of a commission of men. Schools, banks and shopping centers fall within the province of the planners; churches do not.

E.D. Whiteside, the praying man of Pittsburgh, knew this well. Because he realized the futility of man's projects and was utterly dependent upon God, he was greatly used to enlarge the ministry of The Christian and Missionary Alliance. The inspiration of his vision and labors lives today. Every move Mr. Whiteside made to open new branches (churches) was always the result of a previous moving of the Spirit within him as he waited upon God in prayer. This was not planning in the usual sense, but a following of divine leading.

The history of extension is full of glowing triumphs of faith. The details are not the same, but the essentials are all there: a burden of prayer on someone's heart, a vision for a community that its spiritual needs might be fully met and a cooperation of the local people with district and national officers of the Society to gain a foothold. Left to themselves the people in a locality are seldom able to surmount all of the first steep financial barriers. That is the reason for district and national extension programs.

—Rev. Charles E. Notson,
The Alliance Witness,
June 14, 1961

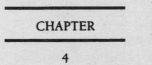

CHAPTER

4

Following the Pattern (Part 2)

The Church grew through the Middle Ages, surviving mighty changes at the time of the Reformation. Yet it grew steadily on. After it had reproduced itself across Europe, it came with the colonists to the New World in the Western Hemisphere. Nine different Christian sects established settlements in the formative years of the colonial era of American history.[1] When the Great Awakening of the eighteenth century swept across England and the American colonies, it created a fertile environment that brought about the birth of thousands of new congregations.[2] The church was so central to family and community life in these early days of America that every people movement meant automatic church planting.

The Early American Church Pattern

In 1835 Lyman Beecher, a well-known Presbyterian and Congregational minister in New England, preached a sermon from Isaiah 66:8

titled "A Plea for the West." In it he called Christians to seize the opportunity to influence the new country emerging in the western American wilderness. He believed that Christians had a duty to shape the religious as well as political destiny of the developing nation. "He called for the preaching of the gospel, the distribution of Bibles, the planting of churches, the establishing of schools and the reform of American morals."[3]

Beecher represented a common interest among evangelicals, whether Baptist, Methodist, Congregational, Presbyterian or Episcopal. This view is typical of the call for a Christian America that historians refer to as "the age of the righteous empire."[4] This sense of corporate mission fueled the church-planting movement that accompanied the American westward expansion.

In time, the Baptists and Methodists far surpassed their contemporaries in church-planting effectiveness. Qualifying for Baptist or Methodist ministry involved far less education than in other denominations, and ministers in these congregations were permitted to serve part time. It cost considerably less to organize a new Baptist or Methodist congregation!

A second factor in their success was the kind of ministers they were producing. "These ministers who worked with their hands along with the frontiersmen appealed to them more than the scholarly Presbyterians. Their crude, highly emotional sermons were well-fitted for the rough conditions of life on the frontier."[5] Pioneering Baptists typically moved in groups, brought their minister with them and began meeting in a settler's log cabin. Later on a church building, also composed of logs, would be erected.

Those Amazing Methodists

Of all the churches, the Methodists were the most successful in planting churches across the western frontier. Calvinist Presbyterians and Baptists (to a lesser extent) emphasized God's absolute sovereignty and electing grace, which included a strong view of predestination, while Methodists, as Arminians, preached the doctrine of man's free will—that man holds his destiny in his own hands. This concept naturally appealed to men and women intent on carving their destiny out of the western wilderness. This doctrine also tended to motivate Methodists to greater zeal in evangelism.

Organizationally the Methodists excelled too. They innovated culturally relevant and effective ministry forms. The circuit-riding preacher, modeled by John Wesley in England, was continued by American Methodists. A traveling preacher who rode on horseback from settlement to settlement could evangelize an entire region. Some circuit riders took several weeks to make their rounds, preaching almost every day, sometimes several times a day. Converts were then incorporated into "classes" led by lay preachers or class leaders where they were taught the fundamental Christian disciplines and doctrines. The result was a remarkable church-planting movement among those frontiersmen who had no church affiliation. In this way, it was not necessary for a group of believers to migrate together to plant a new congregation of the parent denomination.

The chronicling of this movement of church planting across America deserves a full volume of exploration. We must content ourselves here with the telling of a representative story from the Methodist movement.

"We're Building Two a Day!"

George Hunter, a student of John Wesley's methodolgy, tells a story in his book *To Spread the Power* that indicates that God was raising up champions of church planting during these days to assure the forward thrust of the Church.[6] It seems that in the late 1800s the Methodist church was planting a remarkable number of churches, averaging one church a day!

Rev. C.C. McCabe was the director of new church extension for the Methodist Episcopal Church, responsible for planting Methodist churches in Oregon, Idaho and Washington. One day as he traveled by train he read a review of a speech given by Robert G. Ingersol, the famous agnostic philosopher, at a Freethinkers Association of America Convention. In his speech Ingersol declared that "the churches are dying out all over the earth—they are struck with death!"

When the train stopped at the next town, McCabe hopped off and sent a telegram to Ingersol, who was still at the convention. Here is what it said:

> Dear Robert:
> All hail the power of Jesus' Name! We are building one Methodist church for every day in the year and purpose to make it two a day!
> C.C. McCabe

Word of the telegram leaked out and someone wrote a folk hymn that began to be sung throughout the Northwest.

> The infidels a motley band
>   in counsel met and said,
> "The churches are dying across the land,
>   and soon they'll all be dead."
> When suddenly a message came
>   and caught them with dismay:
> "All hail the power of Jesus' name.
>   We're building two a day!
>   We're building two a day, Dear Bob
>   We're building two a day.
> All hail the power of Jesus' name,
>   We're building two a day!"

This song dramatized the frontier Methodists'

quiet confidence in the power of what they offered people. They understood that every church planted rolled back darkness and planted the power of God in the midst of the people. May the Lord raise up a people in our day that will join faith to holy boldness and respond similarly to those who are proclaiming the church to be "struck with death."

The Early Alliance Church Pattern

The Christian and Missionary Alliance was called into being during these days of rapid church planting. Albert Benjamin Simpson had heard the call of God to make seeking Christ's lost sheep his priority. This was evident in the days of his Presbyterian pastorate in Louisville, Kentucky. Simpson had organized an ecumenical cooperative revival crusade which was held at the Public Library Hall and other venues apart from church buildings in Louisville.

Upon the conclusion of these evangelistic meetings, Simpson opted to continue, personally, the Sunday night mass meetings. The local press reported on his decision to continue the public meetings "in view of the widespread desire among the people to hear the Gospel and who do not attend regular church."[7] This observation magnifies Simpson's emerging concern for those unchurched people, many of which had become alienated from the empty formalism of the established church.

It is noteworthy that during these meetings

Simpson and his colleagues innovated special services designed to appeal to narrow "people groups" in the midst of this southern city. A typical Sunday evidenced many kinds of services and appeals. "In the morning each pastor preached in his own sanctuary. In the afternoon a mass meeting was held for black people in Glover's Rink and white working-class people filled Liederkranz Hall. Only young men were given tickets to attend the service in the Public Library Hall. . . . The service in Macauley Theatre was open to everyone."[8]

He took his burden for the poor and unchurched with him to New York City when he accepted the call to pastor the Thirteenth Street Presbyterian Church on December 1, 1879. In New York City, Simpson continued to enjoy regular evangelistic fruit. In fact, his success at evangelism soon set up a crisis in this prestigious church. Some of the members were uncomfortable with the sudden change and "looked askance at the variety of newcomers-poor, shabbily dressed individuals as well as the affluent and educated. To these uneasy guardians of Thirteenth Street Presbyterian's prestigious image, the church's growth was a mixed blessing. How were they to attract their social peers if the church gained the reputation of a city mission?"[9]

Simpson Makes a Choice

When Simpson presented around 100 converts from the Italian quarter of the city—a poor, blue-collar neighborhood—to the church for membership, the crisis came to a head. The church refused his request, and he was forced to commend the new believers to another church for discipling. This was the beginning of the end of his ministry as a Presbyterian pastor. On Sunday November 6, 1881, Simpson preached his last sermon to his congregation from Luke 4:18: "The Spirit of the Lord is upon me because he has anointed me *to preach the gospel to the poor*" (emphasis added).

Simpson's passion to find the lost beyond the reach of established churches motivated him to recruit people of similar passion to join his cause. J.H. Hunter, Christian and Missionary Alliance historian, states that A.B. Simpson was not motivated by dissatisfaction with his Presbyterian church home:

> It was not on any doctrinal grounds that Dr. Simpson severed his connection with the Presbyterian Church; nor is the C&MA the product of division. It was God's Spirit calling His servant to a wider ministry that would embrace the masses at home and abroad. . . . His reach always exceeded his grasp, and this sanctified ambition he imparted to his associates. His zeal, fervor,

love for the lost, and missionary passion he communicated to his followers, and thus built at home a fellowship that is unique in its aims and accomplishments in the sphere of evangelism. General Booth told his Salvationists to "go for the worst." Dr. A.B. Simpson told his associates by precept and example to "go for the masses." It was the masses at home and abroad, the vast host of sheep without a shepherd, which touched his heart and laid a burden on his soul. To reach them, he alerted believers everywhere with the fervor of spiritual truth and the opportunity to be partners in worldwide evangelism. The flame of his own passion for the lost he kindled in the hearts of men and women all over the North American continent.[10]

Beginnings

Simpson left his church when his new converts were not embraced, but he did not abandon the local church as Christ's ordained delivery system for spreading the good news. For Simpson, winning the lost and building and equipping new believers was best accomplished through the efforts of the local church. Within two weeks of leaving the Presbyterian church, he held a Bible study in a rented dance hall following the model of the special services he had conducted in Louisville. In February 1882 Simpson organized his growing following into a new organized church with thirty-five charter members. In the early days of the work, this church planter funded his ministry out of his own pocket.

By 1883 church membership had reached 217, and regular Sunday evening evangelistic meetings were averaging over 700. Growth continued as the church multiplied ministries to reach various segments of the city, always with a view on the unchurched and overlooked. He undertook three major ministries to buttress his evangelistic and missionary passion: a missionary society and magazine to rally Christians to reach the lost in the regions beyond; a "healing home" to provide a place for those suffering from illness and stress to seek God and divine healing; and a missionary training institute in 1883. Of this last enterprise Simpson wrote, "another object contemplated is the opening of a Missionary Training School for Christian Evangelists, where godly and consecrated young men and women can be prepared to go forth as laborers into neglected fields."[11]

Church Planter Extraordinaire

Simpson's bold faith and entrepreneurial spirit are the stuff of which successful church planters are made. In today's jargon, we would say that he was a "developer-initiator." He was able to ask God for guidance, envision a new enterprise, articulate his vision in a general way and then recruit others to help him bring it about. This pattern enabled his ministries to multiply with an effect that far surpassed any reasonable expectation of success. Simpson was not a man of financial means, yet his enterprises found financial support because they were, in fact, God's plan.

Another element of Simpson's success was his ability to transfer his vision for reaching lost people to others and then empower them to reach out and attempt great things for God. Simpson's congregants soon began generating many different kinds of outreaches. The only common factor was that they were focused on evangelism.

> Young men preached on street corners and riverside docks, even carrying their message of reconciliation with God on board anchored ships. Tabernacle members pooled their resources to start a mission on Thirteenth Street. Ladies teamed up for house-to-house visitation and special meetings for fallen women. The South Street Mission was one of at least four havens begun through their efforts. Mrs. Sidney Whittemore began a similar work, the Door of Hope Mission for the ruined women drifting on the city's unfeeling streets. Wealthy tabernacle members gave both time and money to start their own ministries. Mr. and Mrs. Henry Naylor

founded Berachah Mission. O.S. Schultz and his wife funded the Berachah Orphanage for homeless children. . . . The list of activities at the Gospel Tabernacle grew and changed making difficult an inventory of ministries.[12]

When viewed together, these ministries fulfilled Simpson's initial vision for a self-supporting, predominantly middle-class church reaching out to the lost, the hurting and the "Samaritans" around them.

After much hard work and ten moves in eight years, the new church plant was finally rooted as the New York Gospel Tabernacle at Eighth Ave and Forty-fourth Street in October 1889. This location was so well chosen that it continued to serve as the base of operations for the Alliance movement until 1970. Simpson's penchant for reproducing ministry is even evident in his design of this building complex. He included room for a bookstore, classroom facilities for the Missionary Training Institute, dormitory space and his retreat center/rest home, Berachah Home.

The Alliance Develops Unexpectedly!

The early Alliance did not have a master plan for church planting that envisioned and orchestrated movement or intentionally strategized for a certain number of new church plants each year. In fact, building a new denomination appears to have been far from the mind of Simpson. While he had a vision for a reproducing church, he apparently did not envision a new denomination as the result!

> There are cases continually arising where it is necessary to provide special and permanent religious privileges for little bands of Christian disciples who have either been converted in some evangelistic movement or pushed out of their churches by false teaching and harsh pressure and prejudice. Yet these local independent congregations should never be considered as Alliance churches in any technical sense, but simply independent movements which God Himself has specially raised up through the persistent distress and over which we exercise for the time a certain spiritual oversight.[13]

What is remarkable is that these bands, or "branches," as they were then called, continued to multiply as Alliance people reached out to unsaved folks in nearby towns and communities. The fruit of these meetings became the foundation for new "branches."

Another discernable pattern was the "afternoon meetings"—usually held on Sunday afternoons so the group members could attend their own church in the morning—that were conceived as small group meetings for the purpose of pursuing the deeper life (intimacy with God) and support for world missions. These groups, over time, evolved into new Alliance churches. Simpson's passion for knowing God and for extending His kingdom birthed a worldwide church planting missionary movement.

During the early years of the Alliance, there was a clear evidence of apostolic confidence in extending the church's witness through church planting as one after another of Simpson's associates took their leader's passion and direction to their logical conclusions. Many in the early Alliance understood that faith and prayerful planning could catalyze one another.

The Praying Man of Pittsburgh

A good example of this is a man who ministered in Pittsburgh. People said that he was a quiet, frail and weak man. He resisted the positions of honor that were offered him, though he was a man of meager means. He spent long hours sequestered away from his people—but he knew how to pray. In fact, they said that once he sensed what God wanted him to do through prayer, he became transformed into a man to be reckoned with, possessing a holy persistence that would not take no for an answer. He became known as the "praying man of Pittsburgh" for his public commitment to seek solutions through prayer.

This man's name was E.D. Whiteside . . . more affectionately known as "Daddy" Whiteside to those whose lives he touched.

Whiteside's vision for impacting his city extended beyond his own parish. It is said that he and his wife would sit on their urban porch and pray for the city and surrounding suburbs and towns. Map in hand, he asked God to help him extend a gospel witness to these areas. "Show me the steps I must take to see your vision fulfilled," he prayed, "not just here in Pittsburgh, but all around us here in Pennsylvania and to the ends of the earth."

After Whiteside's death in 1927, his prayer book and daily diary were rediscovered. They revealed he had prayed diligently for twenty-eight specific towns surrounding Pittsburgh by name. An Alliance church had been planted in each of them! Daddy Whiteside represents a host of men and women in the early days of the Alliance who fanned the flame of Simpson's original vision.

A Unique Movement

Dr. Louis L. King, president of The Christian and Missionary Alliance at its centennial celebration, concludes a history written to celebrate that occasion[14] with the following retrospective observations.

Dr. Simpson then identified two imperative reasons for the formation of a new religious movement: "The Alliance has its place and calling to lead the people of God farther on into all the heights and depths of the life of

Christ and farther out into all the aggressive work which the children of God have so long neglected. . . . We need to know the standard under which we fight, recognize 'our own company,' and be true to the spiritual trust which God has assigned us."[15]

King reflects:

The Alliance is a unique missionary denomination—a maverick movement into whose soul the Head of the Church breathed, "Go!" from the very start. . . . The Alliance believes that no province or region or country should be exempted from the opportunity to hear the Gospel—witnessing that intends to convert. This is our special trust and we will specialize in it. . . . Our special trust to evangelize at home and abroad therefore finds its source and strength in a very personal imperative: to experience the truth we proclaim, truth that finds its complete expression and fulfillment in Jesus Christ.[16]

Indeed, the men and women of the early Alliance carried on the apostolic commission to "plant the power" of the gospel. The passion and values for this new movement of church planting were embodied in its founder, Dr. A.B. Simpson. It is my conviction that God raises up organizations and movements to bestow a particular redemptive gift on His Church and to fulfill a specific role in extending His kingdom. As that organization/movement ages, the continued blessing of God upon it is contingent on its fidelity to the purposes for which God raised it up. As the Alliance's redemptive gift to the Church is our insight and emphasis upon the Christ-centered "deeper life," so our specific role in the kingdom is to be a church multiplication movement. To the extent that we regain the passion and values that Simpson incarnated, we will know the blessing of God in greater measure in the days ahead.

Notes

[1] According to historian B.K. Kuiper, these groups were Episcopal, Congregational, Catholic, Dutch Reformed, Baptist, Quaker, German Reformed, Moravian and Mennonite.

[2] William C. Tinsley, *Upon This Rock* (Atlanta, GA: Southern Baptist Convention, Home Mission Board, 1985), p. 21.

[3] Bruce L. Shelley, *Church History in Plain Language* (Waco, TX: Word Books, 1982), p. 404.

[4] Ibid.

[5] B.K. Kuiper, *The Church in History* (Grand Rapids, MI: Eerdmans, 1979), p. 354.

[6] George G. Hunter, *To Spread the Power* (Nashville, TN: Abingdon Press, 1987), pp. 19-20.

[7]Robert L. Niklaus, John S. Sawin, Samuel J. Stoesz, *All for Jesus* (Camp Hill, PA: Christian Publications, 1986), p. 11.

[8]I bid, p. 10.

[9]Ibid, p. 36.

[10]J.H. Hunter, *Beside All Waters* (Harrisburg, PA: Christian Publications, 1964), pp. 223-224.

[11]Niklaus, Sawin, Stoesz, *All for Jesus,* p. 58.

[12]Ibid., p. 60.

[13]Ibid, p. 75.

[14]Niklaus, Sawin, Stoesz, *All for Jesus.*

[15]Ibid, p. 251.

[16]Ibid, p. 252.

Voices from the Past

Extension Sunday Is "Church Planting" Sunday

Q. *What is "Extension Sunday"?*

A. Each year Alliance churches set apart one Sunday early in the year to give special consideration to church growth and extension—to planting Alliance churches in the many communities in North America that still do not have a Bible-preaching, Christ-centered church.

Q. *What does it take to plant a new church?*

A. First comes a waiting on God and definite guidance from the Holy Spirit. Then people plant churches as they unite in prayer, in sharing and in giving.

Q. *How good an investment is the United Extension Fund?*

A. One of the very best. Our studies show that new Alliance churches become entirely self-supporting within three years—at most, within five years. On the average, a newly planted church will contribute in missionary dollars in just the first five years what it required to start the church. It's a great investment—it gives 100 percent return within five years!

Q. *What should we pray for on Extension Sunday and in the coming months of 1976?*

A. In 1976 our goal is to start 52 new Alliance churches—that's one every week. We can do it. Our overseas churches are starting three a week. And every new church in North America strengthens this growth overseas.

—Dr. Keith M. Bailey,
The Alliance Witness,
January 14, 1976

Some Pragmatic Considerations

For many years, C. Peter Wagner has stated in his books and seminars: "It has been well substantiated by research over the past two or three decades. The single most effective evangelistic methodology under heaven is planting new churches."[1] While many kinds of evangelism result in "decisions for Christ," each one has a problem with keeping its converts.

Planting Churches Is the Most Effective Means of Evangelism

Billy Graham has probably solicited more decisions for Christ than anyone in history. Yet he admits than only perhaps twenty to thirty percent become responsible disciples of Jesus in a local church.[2] A convert is not truly a disciple until the decision to receive salvation through Jesus Christ's work is followed up with baptism and training to "obey everything I have commanded you" (Matthew 28:19-20). The church—the body of Christ in a given locale—is the best context for discipleship.

The more evangelical churches located in an area, the greater the visibility of the gospel. It is easy to see this "saturation principle" at work in the marketing technique of those who make their living selling hamburgers. How many fast-food restaurants are within a two-mile radius or your home? I can count three near mine—and that's of only *one* chain! Franchise executives know that the best way to meet—and saturate—a community's need for burgers is to build multiple sites, not to continually enlarge the mother store.

Applied to the church, this principle means that multiple churches will provide a more effective saturation of the community with the gospel than a single church could. In fact, a worldwide church-planting strategy called DAWN (Discipling A Whole Nation) is putting this principle to work. Using "saturation church planting," DAWN wants to "see the incarnate Christ present in the midst of every small unit of population in an area, in a country and in the world."[3]

Peter Wagner sees this principle in the work of the apostle Paul. "Part of Paul's influence in the new churches was, undoubtedly, to stir them to evangelize the lost in their cities and to plant new house churches in every neighborhood. No missiological principle is more important than saturation church planting."[4] James Engle and Wilbur Norton, in their book *What's Gone Wrong with the Harvest?* state, "It is a demonstrated principle of church growth that Christianity gains in a society only to the extent that the number of existing churches is multiplied. Multiplication of new congregations of believers, then is the normal and expected output of a healthy body."[5]

How is the making of disciples best accomplished? What is the most effective means of accomplishing the ministry of the church? Keith Bailey, well-known Alliance preacher and leader, answers the question convincingly:

> Planting local churches is the divine plan. The very language of the Great Commission infers the local church. The method for making disciples prescribed by Christ can occur in no other context than that of a local church. . . . When a movement stops planting new assemblies, it declines in evangelistic outreach. Every new church planted enlarges the cutting edge of evangelism. It means that more people will have a direct confrontation with the gospel than if the church had not been planted.[6]

The Church needs to recognize the value of multiple ministries in a community and then apply it to the evangelization of its city and region.

New Churches Are Efficient Disciple-makers

New churches grow better than established churches, say numerous studies of converts, baptisms and worship attendance that compare new churches with older ones.[7] Research done by the DAWN project in England found that "those churches planted since 1989 had grown on average by over 75 percent per year! By contrast, even the strong evangelical/charismatic churches established prior to that date were increasing by just 6 percent a year. In other words . . . the new church plants were growing 12 times as fast as established churches!"[8]

There is much emerging evidence that growth is more likely with less effort in newer churches. The Southern Baptist Home Mission Board has concluded that "If baptism rates per 100 members are used as a measure of efficiency for a church, then young churches are more efficient than old churches. The older a church gets, the less efficient it is in baptizing new converts."[9]

Church Planting Sustains and Expands the Movement

The survival of a denomination demands church planting. Richard Bailey, former district superintendent and vice-president of Church Ministries for the Alliance, has emphasized the need for church planting as essential for the survival of our movement.

> Where are the 100-year old church congregations? Pastors have gone, congregations have changed and most of the buildings that housed them are extinct. Isaiah said it clearly, "Their stock shall not take root in the earth." The church lives only by giving its life to another. . . . Some 32 percent of Alliance churches were not in existence 10 years ago. Had no new churches been planted, we would have only 1,150 churches, not our current number of 1,780. If we opt not to reproduce new churches, at our present rate of closures, we will be extinct in just 42 short years.[10]

Lyle Schaller suggests that at present rates of closure for the American Protestant Church, four new churches will need to be planted for every 100 churches just to maintain status quo!

Peter Wagner makes this bold pronouncement:

> While some denominations have been declining in the United States, other denominations in the same country through the same period of time have been growing vigorously. *Without exception, the growing denominations have been those that*

stress church planting. The leaders of these denominations know that church planting is a central key to their growth, so not only do they believe it themselves, but they see to it that their pastors and lay leaders also believe it. They go to great pains to communicate the challenge of church planting throughout their constituency. They are successful in keeping church planting high on the agenda of their people across the board.[11] (emphasis added)

More Churches Means More Ministry Options for the Unchurched

Each new church provides more options for both the unsaved and the born-again unchurched. It is estimated that as many as 15 million born-again, unchurched people now live in America. The reason given most for their noninvolvement is "nobody invited me."[12] New churches provide options for worship style, philosophy of ministry, ethnic distinctions and social class comfort zones.

There Are Not Enough Churches in the U.S.

Consider the following data. First, the Gallup Princeton Religion Report estimates the American unchurched population to be 195 million. Second, the churches-to-population ratio is declining. There were twenty-seven churches in 1900 for every 10,000 people in America. In 1950, there were seventeen churches for every 10,000 Americans. Today there are only eleven churches for every 10,000 people. Add to these dismal statistics two other facts: 1) the average size of churches in America is under 100 people; 2) many of the eleven churches for every 10,000 people that exist do not preach the gospel.

Another way of visualizing this need is to recognize that in the USA the average city of 50,000 people has approximately 100 churches. If we made an optimistic assumption that 300 people would attend each of those churches there would still be 20,000 unreached people in that city. An accepted rule of thumb among church growth experts is that in America, sixty percent of the population has no church affiliation at all.

The clear conclusion is that there is a desperate need for more gospel-preaching churches in the United States. Church growth experts affirm that this is true in virtually every part of the United States, both rural and urban.[13]

These are five great reasons to involve your church in reproducing healthy Great Commission churches!

Notes

[1] C. Peter Wagner, *Church Planting for a Greater Harvest* (Ventura, CA: Regal Books, 1990), p. 11.

[2] Billy Graham School of Evangelism Lecture, Billy Graham Evangelistic Association, Minneapolis, MN (Lecture attended in Tallahassee, FL in November 1986).

[3] Jim Montgomery, *Then the End Will Come* (Colorado Springs, CO: DAWN Ministries, 1997), p. 20.

[4] C. Peter Wagner, *Blazing the Way* (Ventura, CA: Regal Books, 1995), p. 48.

[5] James F. Engle and H. Wilbert Norton, *What's Gone Wrong with the Harvest?* (Grand Rapids, MI: Zondervan, 1975), pp. 143-144.

[6] Keith M. Bailey, ed. *The Church Planter's Manual* (Camp Hill, PA: Christian Publications, 1981), p. 11.

[7] "How to Plant a Church Seminar," sponsored by the Fuller Institute, Pasadena CA, 1987, seminar notebook, p. 4.

[8] Montgomery, *Then the End Will Come*, p. 28.

[9] Phil Jones, "An Examination of the Statistical Growth of the Southern Baptist Convention," *Understanding Church Growth and Decline 1950-1978* (New York, NY: The Pilgrim Press, 1979), p. 170.

[10] *Churches Planting Churches Manual* (Nyack, NY: The C&MA Office of Church Growth, 1987), p. 25.

[11] Wagner, *Church Planting*, p. 12.

[12] "How to Plant a Church Seminar," seminar notebook, p. 8.

[13] *Churches Planting Churches Manual*, p. 11.

Voices from the Past

We've Come This Far by Faith!

As I snapped pictures of the special occasion, I thought, "What a beautiful church! It's just a year old, yet it's strong and healthy and growing. On top of that it's loving and lovable. And it's *our* baby!"

At the Canby, Oregon, church, Mark 16:15 [KJV], "Go ye into all the world and preach the gospel to every creature," had also meant home Bible studies. Each study group became a nucleus for reaching neighbors and friends around that home. And soon there were many new people coming into the family of God.

As these new believers then began filtering into the Canby church, there was excitement and exuberant life as a result of this marriage between a concerned church and the home Bible studies. And it was a nice feeling for those of us in the Canby church to sense the sweet life of a baby within. Meanwhile the "baby" kept growing bigger.

No one is quite sure just who first mentioned the idea of a church in Oregon City made up of members of the home Bible study groups in that area . . . but it is God's plan for parents to procreate.

On February 15, 1976, the baby was born. It

was a healthy one, with 56 official members and other faithfuls to make the group swell to 111 on its first Sunday in its new "crib."

As I took pictures of the sheet cake on the refreshment table, I thought, "No wonder they chose the slogan 'We've come this far by faith' to put on their first anniversary cake! No one says this first year has been an easy one—they merely say it's been 'beautiful.' "

The new church already has eight home Bible studies of its own. And as a result they too are feeling new life within—just as had happened in our Canby church.

—Isabel Champ,
The Alliance Witness,
July 27, 1977

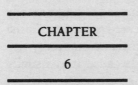

CHAPTER

6

Planting a Daughter Church Is "Great Commission Health"

Lost people need to be saved! Every local church, in fulfillment of the Great Commission, must spread the gospel throughout its geographical area. Acts 1:8 speaks of the Holy Spirit empowering the Church to bear witness in a continuum of evangelism that begins at its door and ends at the farthest corner of earth.

In our American context, Jerusalem speaks of the local community, Judea refers to the county or region, and Samaria refers to the overlooked or despised peoples in one's area who are discovered by observation and by researching demographics.

Efficient and Fiscally Responsible

The most efficient, fiscally responsible and

ultimately effective way to accomplish this task is to multiply congregations—plant churches—at multiple sites throughout one's region.

It is *efficient* because the established church's mission, strategy and resources are intentionally focused on winning the never-reached to Christ and discipling them in Christian community.

It is *fiscally responsible* because it is usually much less expensive than constructing a larger worship facility. A growing Alliance church is faced with limited options: it can multiply its services and cell groups, requiring more paid and volunteer staff; it can expand its facilities to accommodate the increased numbers of people at a cost of $65-$100 a square foot; or it can relocate to another larger campus (the most expensive option!). Wise stewards will give careful consideration to a fourth option: Planting a church, requires a much smaller investment in getting the daughter church started.

It is *effective* because multiple outlets assure saturation of the population with an opportunity to hear and respond to God's offer to them (see chapter 4) .

Birthing a Daughter Church Meets the "Principle of Giving"

The Bible gives us the "principle of giving" as a prerequisite to receiving God's blessing. Luke 6:38 states, "Give, and it will be given to you. A good measure, pressed down, shaken together and running over, will be poured into your lap. For with the measure you use, it will be measured to you."

The first act of giving in church planting is the support of the baby! A mother will provide nurture, guidance and material support until her child reaches maturity. But the dividends of this "giving" are reaped over a lifetime, and the blessings of parenting far exceed the cost.

How well I remember the birth of my first child. My wife Karen and I (she more than I!) soon understood just what the cost was going to be. Our son required constant care, total provision and all the energy my wife and I could give him. Sometimes there was pain and self-sacrifice involved—usually in the middle of the night. But then I reflect on the joy and hours of fun and fulfillment he brought us. We repeated the process three more times! There is great blessing in giving. As our kids grow to maturity, we share in their accomplishments. To see all of them, in their turn, commit their lives to Christ and grow in Him has been a joy. My children and I just finished cleaning up the yard together, and their help made my job easier and more enjoyable.

Likewise, any congregation that will invest its resources—prayer, money, time—in a "baby church" will share in its accomplishments and will gain a partner in its work of world evangelization.

A congregation that will not give of itself for the purpose of reproduction can be likened to a couple who do not want to have a child because a baby would hinder their careers and freedom. Time will reveal that kind of choice to be a very poor one indeed, especially after the novelty of career and freedom have worn off and afford no long-term fulfillment.

Won't It Hurt?

Most will agree with the above conclusions. Yet statistics indicate a low percentage of Alliance churches are intentionally planning to give birth to a daughter congregation. I believe that this is because many church leaders worry about how birthing a daughter church may affect the mother church. Won't the ministries of "old first church" be necessarily diminished if such an event takes place? The answer is surprising to many. There are certain costs and risks involved in giving birth, but experience proves that the result is worth the effort.

Church leaders wonder, "If we plant other churches, won't our church decline?" The following answer is given in the Alliance *Churches Planting Churches Manual*.

According to the best evidence we have seen throughout all denominations, that is not usually what happens. Lyle Schaller, author and church growth expert, observes that where two or more churches of the same denomination exist in one community, the first church has a tendency to continue to grow. This is true of dozens of C&MA churches all over the United States that have planted churches.

The Alliance church in Haverhill, Massachusetts for instance, planted a church in 1984 and another in 1986. During that time, worship service attendance at Haverhill grew from 230 to over 300. Adding the present attendance of the two daughter churches, the number of people attending the Sunday morning worship services has doubled![1]

From all available evidence, this pattern seems to be normative. Peter Wagner estimates that within six months a healthy mother church should have recovered and even gained in the areas of worship attendance and finances lost to the daughter.[2] You will find additional fresh evidence of this is in the planting stories in the chapters that follow.

The Benefits of Motherhood

Alongside this important principle is the observation that there are many invigorating effects within the parent church. Dr. Keith Bailey enumerates several of these benefits:

Another reason for planting new churches is the wholesome effect such movements of new life have on the established churches. Getting involved in planting a new church is stimulating. It challenges the older church to renewal. Planting new churches calls for more manpower. Core lay leaders and clergy are needed from the established churches. That is a healthy condition because it keeps the church at the task of generating and training more leadership.

Some people will be happier and more excited about Christian service in a new church situation. The church that is periodically spawning new congregations will be less likely to suffer internal dissension. The planting of new churches allows for social, economic and cultural diversity to be expressed without the confrontation that comes when all these forces are confined within one congregation.

From a positive stance, to open a new church provides channels for gifts within the congregation or congregations asked to help with the project. Some people do their best in the smaller unit and get uncomfortable when the church grows in size and sophistication. This personality type may have a gift that is suited to planting churches. They thrive on challenges. Their level of faith makes them positive. They are not threatened by informality or unorthodox accommodations often used to open a new church.

The older church is often motivated to new levels of stewardship when participating in planting new churches. By giving a group of active members as the cell for the new group, the finances of the mother church are tested. Not only are the remaining members motivated to better giving—they see the need for growth.

Dr. Hollis Green, authority on church growth in the North American scene, contends that every church contains the seed for other churches. The local church was meant to reproduce itself over and over again. As a healthy plant forms seeds that when planted bring forth other plants, so healthy churches form seeds that produce other churches. There is a price to be paid for the planting of that seed. But there is a far greater price to pay if the seed is not planted. Planting new congregations is a God-given plan for promoting the spiritual health of existing churches.[3]

Dr. Bailey's observation is that birthing can be a wholesome and productive means of renewal and church growth for the mother. It should only enhance the mother church.

The idea that a struggling church will be dragged down by the weight of the effort is simply unfounded. While we have already handled this objection, let me simply add, for emphasis, a viewpoint expressed by Timothy Starr, home missions secretary of the Fellowship of Evangelical Baptist churches in Canada. Starr claims that church planting by daughtering not only reaches a new area but also serves to revive the mother church and train its members.

Most mother churches testify that the space left by those who go to the daughter church is soon filled by new members. Thus two churches experience the benefits of this method and no one loses.[4]

False Beliefs That Hinder Church Planting

False, entrenched beliefs cry out for response. There are virtually an unlimited number of obstacles, objections, concerns and excuses that may be generated; however, these concerns can be grouped into four main categories.

1. *Birthing a daughter church is for the big churches only.*

Elmer Towns indicates the issue is not really one of size but of attitude.

There are several problems confronting this method of church planting, most of which relate to the mother church. While most churches will agree to start a church in two or three years, they are sometimes reluctant to give up tithing members when the specific starting date arrives. Also, some churches are unwilling to give their assets to the infant congregation. A third problem with the mother church is provincialism. Many churches fail to see the need in their own town. They may give thousands of dollars to missions in foreign countries but fail to see the need to start a church on the other side of town. They may argue that the mother church would remain empty if several families started a new church, but *normally the reverse is true.* Both churches experience growth in attendance almost immediately.[5] (emphasis added)

Another issue is the definition of "big church." The average-size church in America is around seventy worshipers. (In the Alliance the average is around 125.) Yet many define "big church" as "bigger than we are!"

The truth is that any size church can be involved in planting another church. Far more territory can be claimed for Christ when churches work together within regions to identify an unreached area and then pool resources to see that new church planted. When a local congregation sees its responsibility as ministering the gospel to "Judea and Samaria" and has passion for reaching lost people, it will work creatively and sacrificially to make it happen. Planting the power of the gospel is not the work of a select few "big churches" but of *every* church!

2. Birthing a daughter church is too big a risk to take.

It is true that some attempts to plant churches do not succeed. Most pastors know someone who was part of a "failed attempt" to plant a church, and some have doubtless become gun shy as a result. I know of a church that at one time was a prolific birthing church, intentionally strategizing new congregations. Because of the failure of one of its daughters, it has pulled back in its zeal to plant the power in recent years. Other people have "heard about" a failed attempt and assume the general success rate of church planting to be much lower than it actually is.

But does anyone advocate stopping witnessing, even though more people reject the gospel than accept it? Do couples stop raising families because their children may die prematurely? Of course not—because *there is intrinsic value in the activity itself!* While the church should desire to succeed in everything it puts its hand to, there is no shame in failing while attempting so lofty an achievement.

The Alliance is committed to encouraging "faith ventures"—activities that require faith and risk to succeed. The Scriptures are clear: "Without faith it is impossible to please God" (Hebrews 11:6).

Naturally we should take some steps to maximize the chances for success of the church plant. Providing coaching and mentoring for the planter and core group leaders prior to the church's launch will go a long way toward raising the success rate. Today there is excellent training available to prepare the planter to meet the critical needs of the new church. The Christian and Missionary Alliance is developing a "systems development" approach to church planting that emphasizes the careful incubation of new churches before they are birthed.

3. *There are already enough churches in our area.*

In answer to this misperception, I refer the reader back to chapter 5. I would also encourage the following exercise.

Step 1: Research the population of your community within a twenty-five-minute drive of your meeting place. This is the effective "drawing area" of your ministry.

Step 2: Total up all the evangelical churches in your community. Find out the seating capacity of each and double it. This assumes multiple services and gives you the absolute maximum number of people that will be able to worship in existing evangelical churches on any given weekend. (Of course this is an optimistic assumption!)

Step 3: Find the number of people that existing churches will *not* be able to minister to corporately—compare the total population of your area (Step 1) with the number of church seats available from Step 2.

This simple exercise will reveal that even if every evangelical church is fabulously successful and fills its sanctuary to capacity twice a weekend, there will still be *thousands* who have no place to sit, let alone belong.

An optional fourth step would be to visit each existing congregation over a series of Sundays and observe the similarity of the composition in each church. Do you see diversity in ethnicity and economic status, or is there a visual similarity among the congregations you visit? What groups of people are being overlooked with the offer of the gospel in your community? They too deserve a church that ministers to them in a way that is culturally relevant and effective at telling the story of Christ.

4. Birthing a daughter church may harm other established churches in the community, thereby violating Christian values of love and unity.

We always want to enjoy the approval of existing churches when a new church is planted—this makes for good neighbors and kingdom cooperation. I like to remind established churches that they too were a church plant at some point. I tell church planters to go to the pastors of established churches in their neighborhood and introduce themselves. The planting pastor can then share his vision for ministry and assure the pastor of the established church that he is after *lost* sheep, not *his* sheep.

Peter Wagner cites an instance of a recent Southern Baptist church planting on Hawaii's Oahu Island. The religious consciousness of the whole community rose. Attendance went up in a nearby Roman Catholic church by 100 percent and by 155 percent in a neighborhood congregational church![6] When a new church moves into an area, it appears that a spiritual force field may develop that can help the churches already there!

Declaring the glory of Jesus Christ and reaping the harvest of souls He has prepared is the work of all true believers and all faithful churches. Anyone who discourages the planting of a new church to partner in the harvest understands neither the concept of Christian unity nor the priorities of our Lord.

One more consideration

There is another issue that, while not a false presupposition, does hinder some from enthusiastically supporting their church's plan to birth a new congregation.

It often goes unstated but nevertheless is a real consideration. It could be stated as simply as, *I don't want to lose the friendship and fellowship group I have grown to love and enjoy.* This is a legitimate concern. The fellowship network, leadership team, choir and practically every subgroup in the mother church can and probably will be affected. However, tough questions need to be answered about the purpose of the church and its amenability to the Lordship of Jesus Christ. Response to this concern can be summed up in the statement, "It's a price that has to be paid." Obedience to the

Great Commission demands it. Recall from Acts 11 the Antioch church's agonizing choice: They too had to give up dear friends—Barnabas and Paul—or disobey the Lord's direct command.

Research into meaningful interpersonal relationships indicates that no one has the capacity to relate to more than twenty to forty people. Any congregation that has already grown significantly beyond that level is already adjusting to being a multi-cell church. Already there are people who attend the church whose names not everyone knows. The congregation has already made the hard adjustments! The congregation can look at the positive side of the change—meeting new people and making new friends.

Conclusion

Birthing churches is an efficient, effective and exciting way to breathe new life into the mother church while expediting the fulfillment of the Great Commission. But timing is important. If the mother is healthy, there is potential for bearing daughter churches. Since the daughter will mirror the mother in many ways, the first priority will be to strengthen the spiritual life of the mother. As an expectant mother prepares herself for the birth of her child, we must seek to prepare the mother with careful preaching and teaching on faith, vision, obeying the Great Commission, utilizing the gifts of the Spirit and an emphasis on corporate prayer life. Every effort must be made to strengthen the mother and prepare her for the time of delivery.

"Church planting is a transmission of life and that life is born of God," says Keith M. Bailey. "It is God who must direct the timing in the birth of a new congregation. From conception to birth, leadership must be sensitive to the Spirit's leading."[7]

Is your church ready to daughter? What should you do next and what process should you follow? A checklist for preparing the mother to daughter follows. It is a starting place for church leaders who want to see their church bear daughters for the glory of God and the expansion of His kingdom.

A General Strategy for Daughtering

The following is a suggested sequence of events that would result in giving birth to a daughter church. Specific times need to be coupled with the accomplishment of each objective. Please keep in mind the value of flexibility: There is implicit danger in both premature delivery of the baby and prolonged pregnancy. The development of the baby should be monitored on a regular basis by the church leadership.

1. Share the vision/solicit group ownership, prayer and support for the goal by the mother.

2. Form a church-planting subcommittee of your evangelism committee.
3. Do demographic study of your general target area.
4. Determine a specific target group/area.
5. Share progress and planning with the whole mother congregation.
6. Find volunteers to be part of the new core group.
7. Find a leader for the group.
8. Begin a core group prayer meeting.
9. Develop a mission statement/philosophy of ministry for the daughter.
10. Hire pastoral leadership/coordinate through denominational channels.
11. Do a target community survey and develop an evangelism strategy.
12. Win new converts from the target area as a verification of God's sanction.
13. Find a meeting place.
14. Set up a separate bank account for the daughter.
15. Develop lay leaders for the daughter's ministry.
16. Organize and incorporate the new group.
17. Elect/appoint leadership for the daughter (see 15).
18. Set a commissioning service date in conjunction with the mother's governing board.

19. Set a date and time for your first public worship service.
20. Sign an emancipation agreement between the mother and daughter.
21. Recognize the daughter as fully self-supporting and independent.

Notes

[1] *Churches Planting Churches Manual* (Nyack, NY: The C&MA Office of Church Growth, 1987), p. 12.

[2] Peter Wagner as quoted in "How to Plant a Church" Seminar sponsored by Fuller Institute, seminar notebook, p. 8.

[3] Keith M. Bailey, ed. *The Church Planter's Manual* (Camp Hill, PA: Christian Publications, 1981), pp. 14-15.

[4] Timothy Starr as quoted in Elmer Towns, *Getting a Church Started* (Lynchburg, VA: Church Growth Institute, 1985), p. 70.

[5] Ibid., p. 71.

[6] C. Peter Wagner, *Church Planting for a Greater Harvest* (Ventura, CA: Regal Books, 1990), p. 40.

[7] Keith Bailey, ed., *The Church Planter's Manual* (Camp Hill, PA: Christian Publications, 1981), p. 55.

Church-planting Testimonies

Voices from the Past

A Decade of Decision

The decade of the '90s will afford unprecedented opportunities for Christian witness and the development of church ministries throughout the United States and Puerto Rico. The Division of Church Ministries believes that by the year 2000 there will be 3,000 established churches in The Christian and Missionary Alliance in the United States. Committees are now at work developing the strategy for making this goal a reality.

The primary purpose of the Division of Church Ministries is to plant and nurture churches. An endeavor to start 1,000 new churches in a five-year period following the centennial is now underway. The purpose is to create, by God's help and for God's glory, a fresh vision, a deeper commitment and a new thrust in every Alliance church to reproduce additional Alliance churches.

The objectives will include: 1) development of a dynamic church-planting lifestyle in every Alliance church; 2) aggressive evangelizing of communities and discipling of believers to be Spirit-filled, maturing, reproducing church members; 3) involvement of 60 percent of established Alliance churches to reproduce a church in a five-year period beginning in 1988; 4) participation of every Alliance church in the evangelization of ethnic minority people and the planting of cross-cultural churches; and 5) discovering, training and developing of both lay and pastoral personnel for church-planting ministries.

Whatever technology is at our disposal must be utilized for the purpose of communicating the continued mission of The Christian and Missionary Alliance, which is to reach the last tribe until Jesus returns. While technology will change, our mission must always be clear and our message unaltered by the changing society of the '90s.

—Rev. Richard Bailey,
The Alliance Witness,
June 4, 1986

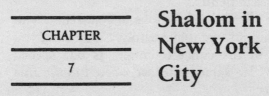

Shalom in New York City

by Patricia Heffernan

It was one of those divine appointments that far eclipsed the difficulties of the day. We were on the boardwalk at Brighton Beach, Brooklyn, distributing flyers in Russian. The flyers announced a free concert that evening at *Dom Melitza*—House of Prayer.

Behind us, with keyboard and microphones, were the six young Russian vocalists. These six young men had come down from Massachusetts to sing and share their testimonies of faith in Jesus Christ. They were giving a preview of the evening's concert to the crowds passing by on the boardwalk.

It was the end of the afternoon, almost time to pack up and head for the church. At first Anatoly passed us by. Then, out of curiosity, he doubled back and looked at our flyer. He could see that some of us were Americans.

"I want to learn English," Anatoly announced in Russian. He told us that he was from Moscow and had been in New York only a few weeks. If he had no knowledge of English, we knew he must be finding the adjustment to America difficult.

"We offer English lessons in connection with our church!" we told Anatoly. "Why don't you come to the concert tonight as our special guest?" He agreed after we offered him a ride with us.

Hungry, Hungry!

From the other side of the sanctuary I watched Anatoly as the group sang and shared their testimonies. He was the proverbial sponge, soaking up the spiritually rich music and testimonies. After the concert, he conversed with several of the young men who had shared their testimonies.

We had planned a meal before the group drove home. We invited Anatoly to join us. His physical hunger matched his spiritual. Ravenously he consumed all that was before him. He must not have eaten in days!

From then on, Anatoly attended the services sporadically until his return to Moscow. We sensed a struggle going on within his heart—that perennial struggle transcending cultural boundaries: Will Jesus Christ be Lord, or will I remain lord? Anatoly knows the issue. The Holy Spirit is drawing him toward salvation. Pray that Anatoly will yet surrender to the Lordship of Jesus Christ.

Sergei

Then there was Sergei. Sergei and a friend also received flyers on the boardwalk that day. They agreed that the concert sounded interesting. That night, there they were! And that very same evening both prayed to receive Christ when the invitation was given. Pastor Gennadiy is now discipling Sergei, who has a deep hunger to grow in his new faith. We hope Sergi will someday be a leader in our church. He hardly ever shows up for church without a friend, neighbor or coworker alongside him. Recently his teenage son prayed to receive Christ. God is truly at work in and through Sergei!

250,000 Others

Some 250,000 Russian Jews have immigrated to New York City. Many of them have come just within the past few years. They have come without financial security. Many are without any family members or friends. Few speak much English.

These Russian Jewish immigrants know what it means to be "displaced." They have left their entire support system behind them. Often the professional skills many of them worked hard to attain are, for the moment, valueless. They must be re-licensed or retrained. All of this requires money, language ability and knowledge of the "system." Doctors become home health aids. Engineers look for odd jobs repairing cars. University professors are glad to work in a retail store.

In many ways things *are* better in America. But for most of these immigrants the shock of being displaced was unanticipated. The experience has left them psychologically and emotionally uprooted. Hope brought them here in the first place, but at present their lives are filled with hopelessness.

For these Russian Jews, America isn't exactly Babylon. But the same God who watched over their forefathers in Babylonian exile knows their hurts and needs. He longs to reach His people through His chosen means—the body of Christ, the Church.

The Messianic House of Prayer

It is into this setting that The Christian and Missionary Alliance has established the Messianic House of Prayer. It was founded to offer hope and new life in Jesus Christ to Jewish immigrants from the former Soviet Union.

Immigrants, whatever their background, are among the most responsive to the gospel. This is especially so for immigrants from former Soviet republics because of the spiritual vacuum created by seventy years of communism.

To reach them, God brought together a ministry team and resources in a supernatural way!

An urban director prayed for an apostle-type who would not only plant a church but develop a church planting movement. Gennadiy Zavaliy is the man. Pastor Gennadiy was a proven church planter in Latvia. God has given him a vision of *dozens* of self-perpetuating churches among Russian immigrants in Metropolitan New York. Pastor Gennadiy's wife, Helen, not knowing why at the time, learned to speak fluent English while living in communist Latvia!

God also added three American workers ready and willing to join the effort. A fourth—trained to teach English as a second language (ESL)—has since joined the team. Just before our church was to open, God provided a Russian Christian pianist to help us get started in a music ministry.

Our first worship service was held June 28, 1997, with just a handful of people. In three months' time, 100 people consider *Dom Melitza* their new church home! For many, it is their *first* church home. We are seeing decisions for Christ on a regular basis.

How Great Is Our God!

In the first few months of its existence, Messianic House of Prayer established a vibrant youth group. It meets weekly for Bible study and fellowship. In August of that first year we held a vacation Bible school. Our ESL classes convene weekly. On the drawing board are detailed plans for a Home Cell Group ministry. We hope to have cells in every district of Brooklyn. Our object is for these groups eventually to become daughter churches.

"Jesus Christ is the same yesterday and today and forever" (Hebrews 13:8). God is doing a mighty work in Brooklyn! He still longs to be a Father to the fatherless and to provide a home to the stranger in a foreign land.

Are We Building Too Much?

The old question of "who should hear the gospel how many times?" is open to debate. We have been told so often that the gospel should not be heard twice by anyone until everyone has heard it once that some dear folk think it has been assigned chapter and verse and slipped into the canon. It is, in fact, a principle with neither New Testament sanction nor common sense basis. I wonder how any readers of the *Witness* mark their conversion from the first time they ever heard the gospel?

We live in America and our initial obligation is still to the people round about us no matter how many times they have heard the gospel. When God gives them up, so can we, but not before. Any congregation that does not weep, pray, witness and—yes—even build churches to reach the people of Hometown has no passion for the tribesmen of Vietnam. If they think they do they are only kidding themselves.

The Christian loves God first and supremely, his neighbor as the logical consequence of this love and the unseen multitudes on the mission field only as a by-product of the first two. The man who does not love the people he sees every day has no love for either the unseen God or the masses, and the Bible admits of no exceptions to the rule.

—Rev. L. Jay Mapstone,
The Alliance Witness,
February 7, 1962

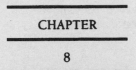

CHAPTER

8

One Youth Pastor's Vision

by Gordon F. Meier

L iving Hope Church was born in the heart of a dedicated youth pastor, Edward E. Dickerhoof. Ed had—and has—a passion to reach lost people for Jesus. When he first telephoned me in the spring of 1995, Ed was rounding out eight years as a youth pastor.

Ed and his wife, Renee, and their six adopted children lived in East Canton, Ohio, twenty minutes from the church they were then serving. But the twenty minutes might as well have been twenty hours. The church he served was in an upscale community. The kids in his East Canton neighborhood, he said, would never be comfortable in his church.

That deeply concerned Ed. He longed to be able to minister to everyday people for whom acceptance didn't mean a particular make of car or a certain brand of clothing.

Ed and I talked for a while and agreed to a face-to-face meeting. When we met, both of us sensed God was drawing us together. Ed went through an evaluation for church planting and, completing that successfully, participated in a church planters' "boot camp."

Ed Becomes an Alliance Church Planter

By the end of June, 1995, Ed had resigned his position as youth pastor and was working full time with the Alliance as a church planter. The East Canton community where he and his family lived was his target. By July he was holding Bible studies and prayer meetings with a good response from the community. Several couples almost immediately began to identify themselves as "regulars."

But what about a meeting place once worship services began? Ed and I considered several options. We eliminated an elementary school because it was old and dark and had only limited parking. A brand-new community center seemed hopeful until we heard what the rent would be!

In late July Ed learned that an old Italian-American social club was to be put on the auction block. On the down side, the building was in bad repair and in a rundown neighborhood. On the up side, it sat on four acres of land and was easily accessible. Inside, the 6,700 square feet were already partitioned off into a large meeting hall, a kitchen, two offices and several classrooms. Out front was an ample parking area. Behind the building was a large picnic pavilion nestled on a wooded lot. I alerted our district's prayer partners to get busy!

Just $77,000 Takes It

On the night of the auction, seventeen bidders turned up. We had arranged for an Alliance realtor to represent us, though none of the local bidders knew of our interest. By the end of the evening, our realtor friend, Dave, had walked away with the top bid: just $77,000! It was truly a miracle. Renee commented that even the numbers of the purchase price were perfect!

It took another $23,000 and hundreds of hours of volunteer work to refurbish the structure. We included a new entrance, central air, new carpeting, some wallpaper. And, of course, fresh paint.

While the building was being readied, the spiritual preparations were going on. Many prayed intensively for the area. We mailed brochures announcing the new church to all residents in the immediate area.

November 5 arrived before we knew it. Ed and Renee and their faithful associates could hardly believe "Birth Sunday" for Living Hope Church was already upon them. Long before service hour, eager, inquisitive people began arriving. By service time, 177 people were on hand!

A Foretaste of Future Blessing

God's blessing in that first service was indicative of what would take place in the ensuing two years. At the time of this writing, eighty people have prayed to receive Christ. Thirty-one have been baptized. Sunday worship attendance is averaging more than 150, and the church is talking of a building program!

Living Hope Church was barely underway when several families from Minerva, twenty miles to the east, expressed interest in having a church there. A part-time assistant pastor at Living Hope felt called to shepherd the group. The church at Minerva opened March 22, 1998.

Living Hope is a "cold start" church—meaning no neighboring church or churches backed it with support and members. It is an especially vivid demonstration of God's power at work to bring living hope into the lives of many ordinary (but eternally lost) people in the East Canton area.

Voices from the Past

Eighty Going on One Hundred

How many new churches are projected for the Alliance in Canada and the United States during 1978? Eighty, responds Rev. Raymond Schenk, Jr., the national extension director for the Division of North American Ministries.

Eighty in '78 will not just happen. There are certain requirements to be met to make each new church a success:

• Prayer—churches are born through prayer.

• Finances—opening a new church costs at least $20,000 during the first year of operation.

• Commitment—churches are begun by people willing to give time and whatever else is necessary to succeed.

Is a new church worth the effort?

"The extension church is the cutting edge of evangelism," says Mr. Schenk. "A recent study of Alliance churches shows that extension churches less than five years old have membership growth two-and-a-half times greater than that of older churches with more than two hundred members."

One of the best ways to fulfill the Great Commission in North America is to plant and grow new churches. Support church extension efforts in your district.

Interview with Rev.
Raymond Schenk. Jr.,
The Alliance Witness,
February 8, 1978

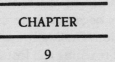

CHAPTER	After
9	Sacrifice
	Comes Joy!

by Linda S. Adams

Many churches hope "someday" to mother a daughter church. Far fewer actually run with the vision. This is the story of a church that did.

Back in 1988, when Doug Jensen visited Oswego, New York, as a pastoral candidate for Oswego Alliance Church, an interesting thing happened. One of the church families drove Doug and his wife, Doris, all over the county, giving them an overview of the area. As they passed through New Haven, a small community east of Oswego, an impression attached itself to Doug's mind. *A church belongs here!* he thought.

Strong though the impression was, Doug kept it to himself—and prayed.

Oswego Calls the Jensens

The congregation at Oswego Alliance formally called Doug to be their pastor, and the Jensens accepted. Although Doug was busy with his new pastoral responsibilities in Oswego, he continued to seek God's will for New Haven. As he became more and more convinced that it was indeed God who had placed the burden for New Haven on his heart, he began to share the concern with his congregation. Gradually a few people caught the vision of reaching the lost in New Haven by planting a church. They too began to pray.

Others in the church were not so sure. How does a church know when to step out and when to be cautious?

From the very beginning, the church leaders' first priority was to have the church united in its efforts. So they planned a series of "explorations." Oswego Alliance teamed up with two other Alliance churches in the region to sponsor a professional demographic study of the area. Also, members of Oswego Alliance took a follow-up questionnaire door-to-door in New Haven. Clearly, a multitude of people in New Haven simply did not go to church anywhere. And God was planting in the members of Oswego Alliance a growing concern for the lost people in New Haven.

Testing the Waters

On Easter Sunday Oswego Alliance held an Easter worship service in New Haven. It gave them opportunity to meet many of the unchurched people there. Later they used the fire hall for a marriage seminar and still later a sportsmen's banquet.

The Oswego members were united in wanting to find God's will. But some of them were not yet sure it included planting a church in New Haven. It was as if God was saying, "Wait. It's not time yet." Meanwhile, the congregation continued to pray.

With the summer of 1997 approaching, leaders at Oswego Alliance challenged the congregation to become "Three-Month Missionaries" to New Haven. They would rent the New Haven town hall and hold regular worship services Sunday morning and evening, a Sunday school and a Wednesday night prayer meeting. Twenty Oswego people responded, including an elder, two deacons, two deaconesses, some Sunday school teachers and others. It was exciting to see how God brought people together.

Cliff Cole was the elder who volunteered. He and his wife, Edie, struggled with the decision. They both were busy with ministries in the Oswego church. But they felt that God was leading them to get involved.

"We had confirmation from the Lord that He had a ministry for us [in New Haven]," Edie says. Both of them have found it a joy to be a part of the action. "The people are really seeking. They are hungry for the Word of God." Cliff leads the worship service and teaches the adult Sunday school class. Edie helps with the music.

A Church That Feeds Them

Harry and Bev Smith are another couple who got involved. They too really wanted to stay at the Oswego church, but the Lord kept urging them on. "It's great seeing people so hungry," Bev says, "who have found a church that will feed them!" The Smiths help out wherever they are needed, whether it is setting up the hall, greeting newcomers, arranging flowers or any number of other things.

"When you see the Lord working in people's lives," they say, "you can't stay away!"

Dan and Mary Douglas volunteered for the summer as New Haven Sunday school teachers. They had been on a short-term mission trip to Mexico and promised God they'd be available "the next time You have a ministry opportunity for us." New Haven was "the next time." They taught the K-5 Sunday school class. Since they home school their own children, they were used to a wide age span!

One special time for Mary was when a four-year-old boy grasped for the first time that Jesus will return. "Really?" he exclaimed. "Wow!"

Perhaps the most amazing part was what was happening in Oswego during the summer. By summer's end, church attendance was higher than before the New Haven volunteers left. Likewise financial giving had returned to its previous level.

Unanimous!

But most gratifying of all was what happened at a congregational meeting held in October. Of the eighty-five members present, eighty-two voted in favor of going ahead with church planting in New Haven. Three members abstained. *Zero* members voted against it! With great joy, the church members listened as New Haven residents at the meeting expressed their gratitude.

For Oswego Alliance, the effort to plant a church in New Haven involved sacrifice. There were many unknowns. The church had to give of its time, its leaders, its money. It risked losing unity, reputation, members. But in looking back, they can see that God has supervised the process and has blessed the church's efforts.

Jesus said, "A woman giving birth to a child has pain because her time has come; but when her baby is born she forgets the anguish because of her joy that a child is born into the world" (John 16:21).

There is great joy in Oswego, New York, as the church celebrates the goodness of God in bringing to life a new church in New Haven.

Voices from the Past

Home Extension Explained

The Christian and Missionary Alliance has long promoted the establishment of new churches in the homeland. In 1952, our latest report year, Alliance Extension established forty-four such new churches. The purpose of home extension is to increase our centers for the evangelization of the unchurched masses. Extension at home means expansion abroad.

—*The Alliance Weekly,*
January 27, 1954

The "Impossible" Dream

by Neysa Costa

L ong before Family Life Center in Birmingham, Alabama, existed, God was planting its seeds in many places. One place was at the 1989 Southern District conference. Delegates, concerned that they were not ministering to African Americans, resolved to plant "four black churches in the Southern District by 1994."

It did not happen, but the resolution stirred a wave of prayer within the district. Surely the dream of a ministry to African Americans in the Deep South was not impossible!

God Rearranges My Plans

In August 1994, I had been on missionary home assignment for almost a year. Normally I would be preparing to return to Burkina Faso, West Africa. My fifteen years of work there was a mix of women's Bible studies, leadership training, children's clubs and back-door nursing that I enjoyed. But Wheaton Grad School had offered me a full one-year scholarship. So I would be studying before returning to Burkina. Or so I planned.

The needs of my African American community in the United States deeply touched me. This time home, it was especially so. I wanted the Alliance to get more involved in urban ministry to African Americans. I longed to see interracial churches where blacks and whites worshiped and fellowshiped together.

I was living at the time in Birmingham—as needy a Southern city as any. I cannot say it any other way: God *led* me to give up my Wheaton scholarship and delay my return to Africa to work in urban Birmingham. What I would do or with whom I would work, I did not know. God spoke to me very plainly, saying, "It is I who will establish your ministry!"

A day after I mailed my request for a missionary leave of absence, the Southern District learned of my burden. Within days they had put me to work as Interim Director of Multicultural Outreach Ministries.

Meanwhile, Prayer

I began my new assignment September 1, 1994. For a year I interned at New City Church and the Center for Urban Missions in downtown Birmingham. I soaked up all the know-how I could get in those vibrant multicultural ministries. They helped me to better picture what *our* ministry would someday look like.

Meanwhile, a small group of prayer warriors gathered every Sunday afternoon to pray for the ministry we ourselves hoped to launch. We prayed for personnel, for a building, for converts. We prayed for a pastor, for a music director, for a piano, for wisdom. We prayed for money. From the beginning, prayer has been the foundation of this ministry.

And in answer to prayer, God brought to us two very key people: Stephen and Dee Manyama. Stephen is from Tanzania, East Africa. When he heard about our efforts in Birmingham, he was pastor of Clarendon Road Alliance Church in Brooklyn. Stephen and Dee were very happy where they were. But they couldn't shake the conviction that Birmingham was in their future.

In June 1995, they contacted Southern District Superintendent Eugene Hall. In August, they visited Birmingham. The Manyamas and we in the district prayed earnestly. In March 1996, Stephen and Dee, sensing both fear and excitement, moved to Birmingham to become part of this new ministry.

A Small Beginning

Even before the arrival of Stephen and Dee Manyama, God had led us to a vacant bank building. It was small but well located. Hard work by many local Alliance people transformed the interior into an attractive large room that could serve selectively as an educational center and a sanctuary.

In his ministry in New York City, Simpson was mindful of the needs of the whole person. We too wanted to touch families where they hurt the most, just as Jesus did while on earth.

On April 1, 1996, we opened Family Life Center. The Center's mission is to prepare urban students and families in Birmingham for success academically, professionally, spiritually and morally. Our classes are in the evening when most adults are not at work and students are not in school. They are taught by our ministry team and by as many as fifteen volunteers from neighboring Alliance and other churches. Among the offerings is tutoring in math and reading and SAT/ACT preparation. We even have a troop of junior Girl Scouts!

With the arrival of Stephen and Dee Manyama, we also got started on the other part of our dream: a worship center that would eventually become a church. In June a core group of us, led by Pastor Stephen, began meeting regularly. Little by little the numbers increased. In addition to Caucasians and African Americans, there are Africans from several countries. This multicultural flavor makes our worship time exciting.

On January 5, 1997, Family Worship Center was officially organized with twenty-one charter members.

We Are Out of Space!

Almost before we moved into that first location, we started looking for our next one! We lacked room. By September I had looked at so many buildings that they were beginning to run together in my mind. We were confident that God was going to provide us with adequate space for our ministry, but we did not have the remotest idea where or how.

Then the call came from Lakewood Baptist Church.

Lakewood Baptist is located in a residential part of East Lake, the same area of Birmingham we had targeted. Like so many inner-city churches across America, it at one time had prospered, building larger to accommodate the crowds. Then came the flight of city dwellers to suburbia. The remaining members, most of them Caucasian, suddenly had more building than people.

When Stephen Manyama and I arrived at Lakewood Baptist Church for our appointment, we were greeted by Pastor E.L. Mullen and lay member David Gardner. They suggested we tour their original building. Although adjacent to their newer, larger facility, it was little used, they told us. They would like to make it available "for a community ministry and to glorify God."

Except for its need of a few "cosmetic" touch-ups, the building was in good condition.

It has a first and second floor, plenty of class-room space, a good-sized sanctuary. Several large rooms could be used for varied purposes. There is a fenced-in playground and plenty of parking space.

We Share Our Dream

Back in the sanctuary of the newer building after our tour, we shared with Pastor Mullen and David Gardner some of our dream. We wanted to see

• the gospel invitation open to everyone regardless of race and socio-economic condition
• cultural diversity a reason for celebration, not division
• the church courageously and boldly become a part of the community rather than to flee it
• families impacted for Christ and urban communities dramatically changed

That kind of passion, we told them, had prompted the Southern District of The Christian and Missionary Alliance to target inner-city Birmingham. That passion had brought together our ministry team. Family Life Center and Family Worship Center were our attempts to tackle a humanly impossible task.

The inner city needed Jesus. But how do you get the attention of people preoccupied by crime, behavioral problems, poverty? It is not easy when people go with the wrong friends, when they lack motivation, when they have no legitimate means of livelihood.

In our minds, we should have a holistic approach. Evangelism and church planting in urban Birmingham needed to be done through community development. We must minister where people hurt.

We Find Some Partners

We sat there in the sanctuary of Lakewood Baptist Church, Stephen Manyama and I, Pastor Mullen and David Gardner. Clearly, we were on the same wavelength. We had the same objectives. We ended that meeting praying together at the front of the sanctuary.

Our second meeting with Lakewood Baptist included their Board of Elders and several from our board. We discussed frankly the implications of using their facility. We were overwhelmed by their generosity. They suggested we lease the building with option to buy. The lease would be for a nominal fee, with no payment until January 1998. After year two, if everyone was still in agreement, they would let us buy the building for much less than its appraised value.

"The Lord has blessed our church," David Gardner explained. "We are not in great need of money at this time. We only want the building to be occupied and maintained by someone with the same heart for ministry that we have. We want the building to be used for God's glory."

We talked also about how our congregations could work together. We could have combined services occasionally. Some of their members might be volunteers at Family Life Center. We could schedule a combined vacation Bible school. The possibilities were many.

We ended that sweet time together by standing in a circle, holding hands, praying and then singing "God Is So Good"!

The Decision Is Unanimous

On Wednesday evening, October 15, 1997, the congregation of Lakewood Baptist Church held a business meeting. A main item on the agenda: To allow Family Life Center and Family Worship Center to occupy Lakewood Baptist's original building under a lease-purchase agreement.

The vote, reported to us later, was unanimous approval! Besides the building, this gracious church family has allowed us to use some of their furnishings as well—tables and chairs, for instance, and cribs for our contemplated daycare center.

We took occupancy on October 31, 1997. November and December were busy months painting, carpet-laying, getting all in readiness. God used the prayers and generosity of many Alliance people to supply all we needed.

On January 4, 1998, Family Worship Center initiated use of the property.

We are still praising God for His provision of

this commodious facility. At first we were concerned because the location was not on a major thoroughfare. But it is in a *neighborhood* and surrounded by *families*—the focus of Family Life Center and Family Worship Center's ministry.

With your prayer support and God's continued blessing, the impossible dream is becoming glad reality!

Voices from the Past

The HEART of Church Extension . . .

The apostle Paul told the Corinthian Christians: "When your faith grows, you will reach out to those around you with the gospel!" Only growing faith and love will give up spiritual vision for our Society's outreach in North America today!

Winning our neighbors at home for Jesus Christ is an important assignment given us by our Lord Himself! Who among us in The Christian and Missionary Alliance can refuse to cooperate in Church Extension and Outreach Evangelism?

Where we are personally committed, we make our investments of time and ability and money. Our pledges on EXTENSION SUNDAY will show the depth of our commitment to planting new Alliance churches wherever they are needed!

—*The Alliance Witness,*
January 3, 1973

Small Town Church Planting

by Jefferson A. Taylor

E very church planting is an original. Some begin as the vision of a single person. Others are the shared vision of several people, or even a whole church congregation. Delmont (Pennsylvania) Alliance Church represents the efforts of many people over many years. We prefer to give the glory to our uncommon God who chooses common people to build His church.

A Part of the Sprawl

Delmont long was known as Salem Crossroads. It was a typical rural community holding tenaciously to its small town charm. That is, until it got caught up in Pittsburgh's suburban sprawl.

Suddenly many families, established in careers and ready to purchase their second homes, were leaving crowded Pittsburgh in favor of Delmont's more rural atmosphere. For the church, it meant one thing: opportunity! People in transition are open to other changes as well. Many who have never given the church a second thought are willing to attend if someone invites them.

The vision for a church in growing Delmont began several years ago. The Western Pennsylvania District's Church Growth Committee took a hard look at Trees Mills Alliance Church. Trees Mills is only five miles from Delmont, but the church itself was isolated. After years of vitality, it was in serious decline. Why not close out Trees Mills and use the proceeds to found a more viable church in growing Delmont?

So a few Trees Mills families began meeting as a Bible study group in the Delmont area. Murrysville pastor Daniel Lawrence rose early Sunday mornings and drove the ten miles to Delmont to lead the study. He did that for four years.

A Pastor of Their Own

In August 1996, my wife, Sharon, and I were invited to meet with the group. We and our two boys, Jonathan and Luke, moved to Delmont that November, ready to start planting a new church.

There are many church-planting models to follow. We settled on the one proposed by Paul Becker in *Church Dynamics*. In brief, it focuses on discipleship. It takes participants through the full continuum: learning how to lead a person to Christ, discipling that person in the teachings of Christ, helping the person discover his or her spiritual gifts, showing him or her how to win still others.

We have also used to advantage Blackaby and King's *Experiencing God* material. The course has increased the vision of our core group.

Summer 1997 was a time of evangelism training and putting our spiritual gifts to work. By then our core group knew how to meet a visitor and lead that person into a relationship with Christ. They knew how to disciple this newcomer and help the man or woman discover and use his or her spiritual gifts.

Numerical and Spiritual Growth

Numerical growth as well as spiritual growth is evident. When Sharon and I arrived in November 1996, the group numbered less than twenty. For the last quarter of 1997, average weekly attendance was forty-two.

We are renting a building that once was Delmont's Catholic Church. Several years ago, the congregation built a much larger facility. A couple of people who felt especially attached to the old building bought it. They did some renovating of the interior, planning to make it an office building. But they never marketed it. When Pastor Lawrence approached the owners about renting their property, they were delighted to see a church use it.

We will soon need to remove some partitions to enlarge our meeting space. In 1998 we will begin a building fund and start looking for a more permanent site.

But property and even numerical growth are not our primary aims. Delmont Alliance Church is content to allow God to bring those things to us when and as He will. Right now we are concentrating on Jesus' command to make disciples—to reach our community with the good news of Jesus Christ. Our desire, in the words of Colossians 1:28, is to "proclaim [Jesus], admonishing and teaching everyone with all wisdom, so that we may present everyone perfect in Christ."

Voices from the Past

Things You Wanted to Know about Alliance Extension

Renewed emphasis on extension in The Christian and Missionary Alliance has brought such terms as "Key City Project" and "Revolving Fund" to the fore. To answer your questions about all of the various facets of extension work, a vitally important link in the comprehensive program of the Society, *The Alliance Witness* has arranged an interview with Dr. Kenneth Berg, extension secretary under the Home Department.

Question: *On what premise is money from the General Treasury set aside for such a purpose?*

Dr. Berg: It is the feeling of the Board of Managers and the Home Department that the building of new churches is essential to the future of missions. We now have over 1,100 Alliance churches in the United States and Canada, and more than 800 missionaries. Therefore, every time we establish a new church we are in effect sending another missionary to the field.

Question: *What has been your main concern as you have traveled across America in behalf of Alliance extension work?*

Dr. Berg: My main concern is that the Alliance in general might become more extension-minded. I have been very much disturbed by the lack of interest in reaching out with the gospel.

Question: *What message would you leave with every member of the Alliance?*

Dr. Berg: Our Society is at the crossroads. If we are to do our work well as a great missionary organization—in God's sight—we must strengthen the home base by continually expanding and extending our ministry in the homeland. May we all join hands together by praying, planning, working and giving to insure the growth of our witness.

—David R. Enlow,
The Alliance Witness,
May 6, 1959

	"Attention,
CHAPTER	Shoppers!"
12	*by Linda A. Thomas*

An older gentleman was walking through Saratoga Mall in Saratoga Springs, New York. Suddenly he stopped to scrutinize the name over one of the storefronts. "New Life Fellowship," it read.

"New Life!" he remarked to Karen Wood, working at a desk just inside. "At my age that's a contradiction of terms!" Karen immediately thought of Jesus' conversation with Nicodemus, who wondered how he could have new life at his age. She knew God was giving her another opportunity to share the gospel. She used the man's own comment as her entree.

A Church in the Mall?

The church-planting effort in Saratoga Springs wasn't planned to be in a shopping mall. Pine Knolls Alliance Church in South Glens Falls, New York, called Joel Smith to take on the job. True, the steering committee wanted to reach the unchurched where they were. And "where they were" happened to be in shopping malls. But the committee had in mind something more conventional.

The committee looked at properties for sale, vacant buildings for rent, a room at the public library, a gym, a public school. All had some major detraction—too expensive, poorly located, too many restrictions.

Even when space at Saratoga Mall came into the picture, the going rate was beyond their means. Then, unexpectedly, a creative mall manager made an offer the committee could not refuse. Since the mall had unrented space, he was willing to negotiate an affordable rent just to increase mall traffic. Coming from a religious background, the manager respected what the group was trying to do. Besides, having a church in his mall would be a service to the community. He was even willing to let them have free use of other unrented space for a children's church.

Pastor Joel remembered a vision God had given him years ago of praying with people in a mall. Suddenly everything was falling into place! Surely this was the Lord's doing.

New Life Fellowship held its first service in Saratoga Mall on March 3, 1996.

The Church behind the Church

How it all started goes back a bit in time. Pine Knolls Alliance in South Glens Falls, the "mother" church, had a problem. A good problem. It had more people than space! The congregation was challenging Pastor Scott Borden to find a way for the church to grow. Not that Pastor Borden needed the prod. He was already seeking God concerning the next step. And God seemed to be nudging him to plant a church in the Saratoga Springs area.

"The church was on fire about the idea right from the beginning," Pastor Borden recalls. A number of the members at Pine Knolls Alliance lived in communities twenty minutes or more from the church. A church in the Saratoga Springs area would put an Alliance church nearer to many of them.

Some eighty people from Pine Knolls Alliance decided to become part of New Life Fellowship. Members of the steering committee became the leadership team, together with Joel Smith. Many others stepped forward to take various positions of responsibility.

From the first, community response in Saratoga Springs was strong. Sunday morning worship attendance hovered at the 180 mark—eighty percent of capacity. Every week, children's church leaders had to make room for more new children.

What Will People Say?

Karen Wood, the former volunteer church secretary, probably had more opportunity than anyone to monitor the public response to a church in the mall. Sitting at her desk near the entrance to the church's space, she heard the comments.

"People's reaction to seeing a church in the mall ranged from 'That's neat!' to 'That's weird!' " she says. On the whole, however, sentiment has been positive. The local newspaper ran a full-page feature story on New Life Fellowship. Instead of burying it in the religion section, they positioned it prominently on the third page.

"The church's presence in the mall helps people 'connect,' " says Pastor Smith. "They will walk in and ask what we're about, and they'll take literature."

Pastor Smith tries to make sure they get much more than a tract or a brochure. He wants the public to see New Life Fellowship as flesh-and-blood people who love others with Christ's love. He wants to be sure someone is on hand to share the good news of Christ in a relational way. This, together with the church's mall location, helps to dispel the popular notion that the church is a building.

Not only Pastor Smith but the other staff members as well put the emphasis on God's love. They want to love people to the Lord. They want to use the gifts God has given them. They are at the worship center during the week to answer questions and to pray with people.

And God directs needy people to them.

Service with No Strings Attached

New Life Fellowship has undertaken several outreach projects—with no strings attached. One Saturday about fifty people of all ages enthusiastically washed 120 cars in four hours—for free! On another Saturday, with a mall trade show in progress, Debbie Smith, wife of Pastor Joel, organized a cotton candy giveaway. "Sweet, Pure and Free," the sign read. "Cotton Candy and God's Love." That day Debbie led a forty-year-old man to Christ. He said God had been telling him he needed to find a church. And here was a church right in the mall!

Debbie has discovered that servant evangelism starts with love. It lets people receive the truth in a natural and relaxed way, the way Jesus operated. To be effective, servant evangelism must be covered by prayer. Then God can use simple things to show Himself powerful.

At New Life Fellowship Pastor Joel has encouraged the ministry of cell groups. He wants each member to develop his or her spiritual gift. Ministry, in Pastor Smith's mind, goes hand-in-hand with relationships among Christians. All believers need to be part of a ministry team where gifts and relationships can function together.

"My biggest thrill," the pastor says, "is to see people come to know Christ and then reproduce their faith in others." He encourages each member to ask two questions: "Whom can I reach out to?" "How can I help that person develop his or her relationship with Jesus Christ and His Church?"

Spiritual Ministry in a Secular Setting

When Jesus spoke to the Samaritan woman, her life was transformed. And it happened in a very ordinary setting—at a well. Jesus witnessed to the woman where she was.

Today the Spirit of the Lord ministers in the secular setting of Saratoga Mall. With God's help a group of believers has planted a thriving church by proclaiming Christ in an unlikely place.

In two short years Sunday morning worship attendance has climbed to the 300 mark. New Life Fellowship has had to move twice within Saratoga Mall. It now occupies five times the original space—still at an affordable rental rate. Truly the Spirit of the Lord is at work!

Church Extension Comes to Life

A spirit of extraordinary faith has characterized The Christian and Missionary Alliance from its inception. It is small wonder that The Christian and Missionary Alliance occupies a position of honor and respect among the leading missionary societies of the world.

The pioneer outreach abroad has been accompanied with a more gradual enlarging of the fellowship in the homelands. While there has been no intention of shirking responsibility at home, the establishing of new churches on this continent has been largely left to individual initiative. Having seen instances of certain fine church organizations losing their passion for missions abroad when they began making of themselves strong denominational institutions, Alliance people have an understandable dread of being deflected from the course in the same manner.

As a consequence any proposals for expansion to be directed through the Society's administrative headquarters have been either squelched or severely limited by crippling restrictions. The opposition always arises from the determination to protect the missionary dollar. Not that opinion is seriously divided on this. Everyone wants to see more Alliance Churches established. At the same time everyone sees the threat to the character of the Society if missionary money is appropriated for this purpose.

The result has been that those who have an interest in starting new churches have had to forfeit many promising opportunities. They have not been able to count on sufficient financial backing from the Society. To a faithful family or two on the scene in a given locality, the reasons for having an Alliance church may be very clear and urgent. Sometimes the district office may be in position to offer them some encouragement. But concern for getting things started appears then to vary inversely as the square of the distance from the place in question. At that point some church organization that has money to spend on an extension project usually takes over. The little nucleus is absorbed into that program which then benefits by their gifts and abilities.

Since their heart interest is with the Alliance they cannot be wholly content, and yet they have a feeling that their beloved Society has let them down. What might have become a center of missions and evangelism becomes another trophy of denominational enterprise. Another community that might have had the full-orbed presentation of the gospel in its fourfold character is closed to the message and vision of the Alliance. Where there should have been a church that would share in the special calling and ministry God has given this Society, a different sort of ministry prevails.

That is the reason for this article. Everyone should know that he can have a part in putting new vitality into this great undertaking.

Establishing new Alliance churches will insure our keeping pace with penetration into unreached territories. That same pioneer spirit must be as much a part of our expansion at home as abroad. Simply raising money in support of ministries on the foreign scene does not mean that a church is fulfilling its calling as part of this Society. We have an urgent responsibility to people in the homelands. Our growth has lagged disgracefully behind the population increases on this continent that have come since The Christian and Missionary Alliance was born. A complacent attitude toward neighborhoods, cities and regions about us that lack a vital gospel witness is incompatible with the nature of this fellowship.

—Charles E. Notson,
The Alliance Witness,
April 20, 1960

<table>
<tr><td>CHAPTER
13</td><td># The House That *God* Built</td></tr>
</table>

CHAPTER	**The House**
13	**That *God***
	Built

by Jody Brown

H i!" said the male voice on the other end of the phone. "I just wanted to welcome you to the area. You'll soon realize that your church-planting efforts are going to fail. Especially since you're meeting in the chapel of a psychiatric hospital. People will not worship there."

That was the "greeting" from a local church leader who had an office in the same building where my husband, Jeff Brown, had set up ours. But the man did not know that God had already given us His promise in Jeremiah 32:27: "I am the LORD, the God of all mankind. Is anything too hard for me?"

The Lord Was Leading Us

After a two-year term at the Evangelical (International) Church of The Christian and Missionary Alliance in Bangkok, Thailand, God was clearly leading us to plant a church. It required a huge leap of faith. The majority of my husband's ministry had been with teens. Although he had neither read a book on church planting nor taken a course in it, God had put church planting on our hearts. The Great Lakes District of The Christian and Missionary Alliance sensed our call and decided to let us try.

So in the spring of 1992 we loaded our U-Haul and moved to Grand Rapids, eager to "go and make disciples."

From the beginning, it was not your typical church-planting operation. The Great Lakes District bought an eight-acre parcel of land and a four-bedroom parsonage. It made an immediate statement to the community: We were there to stay!

Ours was not the first Alliance attempt at church planting in Grand Rapids. The initial vision began in the mind and heart of Dee Laetz, a Grand Rapids woman with an Alliance background. She called the district and asked if a Bible study could be started in her home. She hoped it would lead to a full-blown Alliance church.

Once a small core group had assembled, the district brought in a pastor. After about six months, he left discouraged, feeling that Grand Rapids, with its over 600 churches, didn't need another. Yet a detailed demographic study concluded just the opposite. Approximately fifty percent of the community was unchurched.

There was plenty of room (and need).

We rolled up our sleeves, ready to go to work!

A Disappointing Start

When we announced our first worship service May 3, 1992, we hoped the small core of believers—some thirty people—from the first attempt would show up. That did not happen. Jeff preached to a handful of adults while I taught our two young children in the basement. Convinced of God's call, we pressed ahead.

Because the district was fully supporting us, we were able to focus all of our time on church planting. Our big question: Where do we begin? We decided to send out an attractive, contemporary mailing introducing ourselves, our church and The Christian and Missionary Alliance. To personalize the mailing, we had all 20,000 pieces hand-addressed.

To our surprise, the mailing drew a very small response. But we did attract a few families who, in time, became key families. We continued with several other mailings throughout the year. Most of our visitors, however, came through word-of-mouth invitations and family networking. By the end of our first year, Crystal Springs Alliance Church (as we named it) had sixty regulars attending. Forty of them were not worshiping anywhere the year before.

The Stomach Route

We continued to network throughout the community, meeting as many people as possible. We prayed that the Lord would direct us to "open" people, and He did. After making a hopeful contact, we invited the person for dinner. Over a five-year period, I cooked a "company" meal at least once a week and many times twice a week. It was a great opportunity to get to know some wonderful people. It also acquainted us with the local felt needs. Not all who came to dinner became part of Crystal Springs Alliance, but the church began to grow.

Beginning our very first Sunday, we scheduled a time of fellowship after every worship service. It was never easy to hurry out the door after our worship service! Fellowship time included a "mini meal." It made an easy transition for visitors and gave us time to get to know one another.

We worked hard at not being a "typical" church. We ingrained into our people the need to wait and get acquainted. We trained our members in how to greet newcomers. Each family took turns bringing the "mini meal." This complemented our philosophy that everyone should have a ministry responsibility, just like chores in a family. People rotated on the meal schedule, the nursery, the set-up crew, teaching, cleaning toys, and on and on. No one person did it all, and no one burned out.

A Balanced Schedule

If you looked at our yearly calendar, you would see that it divided into five balanced areas: prayer, Bible study, outreach, service, fellowship.

One Sunday night each month we held a two-hour *prayer* meeting. For many of us, it became the highlight of each month. It was well attended because my husband made it a priority. We prayed for missionaries, we prayed for those we were trying to reach, we prayed for continued unity in the church.

Both men and women had a weekly *Bible study*. We also had specific interest studies such as "Strengthening Marriages." Our goal was to have seventy percent of our adults involved in a Bible study. We stayed consistently close to that goal.

Outreach efforts were continuous, from organized Christmas coffees to backyard events and adult board game nights. We even sponsored a self-defense class at which a police officer gave his testimony. Our outreach efforts were aggressive and intentional.

"Servant" evangelism (doing random acts of *service*) set us apart from many area churches. We decided to hit head-on the negative attitude nonbelievers in our community had toward Christians. We did free (no donations accepted) car washes, a community rummage sale in which everything was free, free

Christmas gift wrapping through a local K-Mart. We picked up trash after a local parade. Things like that expressed God's love in practical ways. We wanted our reputation to be pure and inviting, representing the love of Jesus.

Fellowship made us a family, whether it was the annual canoe trip, a churchwide summer camp out, community Christmas caroling or working together to paint someone's house. These fellowship times helped to build a strong congregation. As the familiar chorus says, "They'll know we are Christians by our love."

Uncompromising on the Word of God

When it came to the Word of God, we were very conventional, very traditional. God's Word was never compromised. Pastor Jeff did not preach feel-good, everything-is-all-right-in-your-life messages. The Word of God came alive through his expository sermons and real-life applications. God's Word was central to all else we did. Our ministry in Grand Rapids was built around it.

Jeff was always very mindful that he preached *two* sermons each week: the one he delivered Sunday morning and the one he lived out Monday through Saturday. Integrity before others and before God was Jeff's top priority. And God used that discipline for His glory in the church.

Each week we issued a newsletter. We looked upon it as our "mid-week glue," for communication was another high priority. Everything that was going on or about to happen was reported through our two- to four-page newsletter that we mailed to everyone in the church. It required a lot of work, but it kept the ministry momentum going. The dividends were well worth the effort!

Today Crystal Springs Alliance is a dynamic, growing, self-supporting church that is quickly becoming the largest Alliance church in Michigan. It is a living testimony to God, who tells us to be faithful to Him and He will build His Church. Even if some nay-sayers tell you otherwise.

What an awesome God we serve!

We Have a Responsibility to Our Cities

At present The Christian and Missionary Alliance is working in more than thirty-five inner city situations. There are twenty-one Spanish-language churches, seven Negro congregations, a witness to the Jews in three areas, four Chinese churches, and one congregation each of American Indians, Japanese, Jamaicans and Koreans.

We are making plans to penetrate farther into the spiritual vacuum of the inner city by establishing additional new ministries. At the very least we must double our inner city work in the next five years.

We should not curtail the work we are doing abroad. We cannot. But neither can we relegate to others the responsibility of helping the people of our own land. Ever-increasing numbers of people crowding into our large cities make it imperative for us to expand and broaden our work and our witness.

—Rev. Leslie W. Pippert,
The Alliance Witness,
November 20, 1968

To Heal a City

by George Reitz

I t began for David Beidel as a prayer request. The request came from a young man temporarily living with David and his wife, Rebecca, in their Staten Island, New York home. Would they pray for his ten-year-old niece? She was being sold as a prostitute by her stepfather to support his drug habit.

Of course David and Rebecca prayed. But God began to grip David with the pervasive iniquity in every area of Greater New York, including Staten Island. The horrors of thousands of abandoned and abused girls and boys flashed before his eyes. He sobbed uncontrollably.

"Lord," David Beidel cried out, "use me to heal my city!"

A Modest Beginning

Two years later, in February 1992, New Hope Community Church had its beginning in David and Rebecca's living room at 245 Van Buren Street. Seven others were present at that first meeting. It was not exactly the kind of Christian army needed to take a city for Christ. But they were two more than A.B. Simpson started with in Manhattan more than a century earlier.

Initially, two ideas converged. They would need a surrogate family structure to bring healing to countless city dwellers who came from dysfunctional, abusive homes. Therefore they determined to develop a cell-type church, geared to effective one-to-one nurture.

But there was another dimension. David himself was a second-generation believer. For some ten years he had worked in a church comprised largely of Asian second-generation Christians. He saw the potential of these grounded, talented Asians—if only they had a vision of the needs around them. A wedding of this resource group and the many homes in dysfunctional pain could be extremely effective.

New Hope Community Church soon outgrew the Beidel living room. The church rented space at First Presbyterian, but it was somewhat out of the target neighborhood. Early in 1995 the congregation discovered Veterans Memorial Hall on the grounds of Snug Harbor Cultural Center. The place was in their neighborhood, and it has proved to be a viable, functional alternative.

Hands and Feet for Jesus

This exciting, multiethnic congregation in the New Brighton section of Staten Island now averages 150. They call themselves "a house of hope in a world of pain," for New Brighton is often described as drug infested and hopeless. They want to be Jesus' hands, feet, eyes and voice in a transitional community.

They believe the best way to carry out their mission is by "taking one block at a time." They cite the method of Nehemiah, who restored Jerusalem's walls as citizens rebuilt the section nearest them. Each "builder family" is to take responsibility to pray for and seek the healing of its own block.

Twice each year "Sunday service is 'Service Sunday.' " On that Sunday the members fan out to their blocks to serve the felt needs there. They publicize their availability for the entire day. It may be to provide basic help for widows, single mothers, the elderly and disabled. It may entail light carpentry, lawn cleanup (yes, there are yards in New Brighton), cleaning out gutters. It could be area beautification, even minor auto maintenance. The members' hope and prayer is that people will see a small fraction of the love that Jesus Christ has for them.

The secret of New Hope Community's growth lies in its vision, its networking and its community focus. The vision is big—as large as New York City!

Project Hope

In practically every American inner-city community, New York City included, the low income housing projects are centers of corruption. New Hope Community Church reasons that if an area's housing project can be reached for Christ, the whole neighborhood will follow. For New Hope, the nearby Jersey Street and Markham Gardens housing projects were a logical starting place. The church named its plan Project Hope.

Most people who become Christians do so between ages four and fourteen. Knowing this, the church has targeted that age group in a Markham Gardens assault. It uses the housing's recreation room to coordinate such planned events as basketball leagues, tutoring programs, youth choirs, special events and a youth group. The members of New Hope have positioned themselves in the center of the project's community life.

Aware that there are some believers already among the residents, the church has called for united prayer for the healing and transformation of the housing project. They feel God blesses true Christian unity with a special outpouring of His Spirit.

To lead Project Hope, the church hired its second staff member, Willie Alfonzo. Willie understands well the "ins and outs" of the projects. He has been there. One of his major missions is to develop a church within the housing project.

There is a basic, documented dynamic when

God saves people in these city housing projects. Once they are reached and transformed by the gospel, they leave the poverty of the projects. This "redemption lift effect" means that to keep an effective, sustainable ministry in a housing project requires an intentional strategy.

Procreation Is Genetically Encoded

New Hope Community Church understood this dynamic. But New Hope was born with church planting in its genes! It knew that any church planting in the housing projects would need to recognize the special dynamics of upward mobility. For the new church in Markham Gardens Housing Project to be sustainable long term required a unique, interfacing relationship. As believers left the project for better housing, many would feel more comfortable in the mother church—New Hope Community. The project church thus would become a feeder for the mother church! And New Hope, in turn, must need to continue to encourage trained, mature members to be an intentional part of the project church. Otherwise the project church would not remain effective and sustainable. This symbiotic relationship is a critical component in project-type church plantings.

From the beginning, New Hope Community has recognized that winning a city to Christ must be a cooperative effort. So it determined to network to get the large job done. It has endeavored to recruit area Christians and instill in them its vision. New Hope encourages these believers to remain in their own churches while working to bring healing to their city blocks.

Pastor Beidel has used a local cable TV station to help publicize his vision. And the church looks upon area college campuses as fertile recruiting grounds. Nyack College has fielded a Staten Island gospel team of students. The church is hoping interns from Alliance Theological Seminary also will help. The broad, passionate vision of David Beidel is driving this recruiting engine.

The Body of Christ on Purpose

New Hope Community's emphasis on making a difference in its community is causing the church to grow. It is attracting people who are tired of the business-as-usual, let's-care-for-ourselves approach to church. New Hope Community offers a no-nonsense brand of servant evangelism, one that everybody can be involved in. Its goal is for the church to be the church in its neighborhood and on its city blocks.

New Hope Community believes the church is called the body of Christ for a reason. It is meant to be the hands, the feet, the eyes, the ears, the mouth of our Lord Jesus. By God's grace and empowered by His Spirit, it is exactly that to the lonely, the broken, the despairing.

Voices from the Past

Training for Church Planters

In recent years the Alliance, along with many other evangelical denominations, has made a strong commitment to starting new churches across North America. The planning for the C&MA's centennial advance, for example, includes the strategy that about half its growth will come from newly planted churches.

—*The Alliance Witness*,
March 27, 1985

It All Started One Summer

by Gordon F. Meier

More than a hundred years ago, the message and ministry of Albert Benjamin Simpson reached the city of Cleveland, Ohio. Several Christian and Missionary Alliance "branches" (as they were called then) were established in various areas of the city. Some of them were comprised of African Americans.

From one of those African American congregations came the Cleveland Colored Quintet of national and international fame. Later, Dr. Howard O. Jones, who would become an associate evangelist with the Billy Graham Evangelistic Association, was the pastor of that church.

Hard Times in Cleveland

But the African American Alliance churches in Cleveland fell on hard times. By the late 1950s, only the Union Avenue Alliance Church remained—a merging of two other congregations. For the next forty years, Union Avenue was the only African American Alliance congregation in a city demographically fifty percent African American. The Central District, under whose jurisdiction Cleveland falls, was not content with that status.

We challenged our district's 1,000 Prayer Partners to pray. We needed wisdom as to how to plant Alliance churches among the large African American population of our district—including Cleveland. Was a new strategy needed? Where would we find church planters? And money? How could the Alliance break into the African American community?

About that time, the district began what we call our "Church Planting Summer Internship Program." The idea is to place a ministerial student (from a college or seminary) in a district community during the summer. In that time the intern would test the spiritual responsiveness by relating to people in the community, beginning a Bible study, holding backyard Bible clubs for children, sponsoring outreach events. These activities had one goal in mind: to lay the foundation for a potential new church.

Enter Ron Morrison

As we were completing the details of this program, Ron Morrison telephoned. He said he would like to get acquainted. He had been talking with Rev. Alfonso Tyler, executive secretary of the African American Pastors Association of The Christian and Missionary Alliance. (Mr. Tyler, it turned out, thought Ron would make a great Alliance pastor.)

From our very first encounter, Ron Morrison proved to be a warm, sincere layman. For twenty-one years he had been employed at Lincoln Electric in Cleveland. But he sensed that God might be leading him into full-time church ministry. So he was in the process of completing a theological program through correspondence. His wife, Anita, was a woman of unusual spiritual depth and warm relational skills. She had a burden to reach people for Christ and see them mentored and discipled.

The upshot of all this was that in the summer of 1995 Ron became our first summer intern. It meant a three-month sabbatical from his employment with no guarantee as to what would happen after that.

Immediately, Ron and Anita began reaching out into their southeast Cleveland district, a racially mixed area fifty percent African American, fifty percent Caucasian. Ron began two Bible studies, one in their home and another several miles away in the home of a friend. The Bible studies started small, but they quickly grew. While some unbelievers attended and showed real interest, a large number of believers without church homes also came. Clearly there was a tremendous need for solid Bible teaching, leadership development and consistent discipleship. These people were hungry for deep spiritual truth.

In addition to the weekly Bible studies, Ron and Anita held "kids' clubs," sponsored picnics and arranged fellowship gatherings. By the end of August, just twelve weeks after the internship program was initiated, we rented a church on a Sunday afternoon and held an "Interested Persons Meeting." More than fifty people attended! Many of them pledged their commitment to a new Alliance church, should one be established.

Time for Action

With interest like that, we acted! Ron resigned from Lincoln Electric to begin as an Alliance church planter. Six weeks after that initial meeting, Hope Alliance Bible Church held its first service. It was held Sunday afternoon in a rented Baptist church with 125 people attending. And at the end of that very first service, a man gave his heart to Christ!

For the next fifteen months, forty to fifty people met regularly each Sunday afternoon. But neither the time nor the rental arrangement was satisfactory. Clearly Hope Alliance needed a place where it could reach out in ministry seven days a week. Again we asked our prayer partners to intercede.

Early in 1997, Pastor Morrison learned that the Slovenian Home would be available at auction. It was a large building—7,600 square feet

in all—and well maintained. Upstairs was a social hall that was rented out for wedding recep-
tions, reunions and polka dances. Downstairs
was a dining room and a full bar open daily to
members of the Slovenian Club. Two parking
lots and a small house completed the property.
Located in Maple Heights, even closer to the
center of Cleveland than their rented meeting
place, it seemed ready-made.

After much prayer and discussion between
church and district, we submitted a bid. Our
bid was not the highest, but our offer of a cash
settlement tipped the scales. Hope Alliance
Bible Church had its building!

Palm Sunday afternoon, March 23, 1997, the
building was dedicated. More than 300 people,
including guests from seventeen district
churches, attended. Although it was a time of
celebration, for once in the former Slovenian
House no alcohol flowed and no one danced
the polka!

God's Blessing Continues

Since then, God has continued to bring new
families and individuals to Hope Alliance. There
has been numerical, financial and—most importantly—spiritual growth. Although all of the initial core group was African American, part of
their vision was to establish a multi-cultural
congregation. They are seeing this objective fulfilled. At least six Caucasian families now par-
ticipate in the church, serving in various ways.

From the beginning, this congregation caught A.B. Simpson's missionary passion. In its first year, the church contributed twenty percent of its total receipts to the Great Commission Fund. In the church's second year, it held *two* full missionary conferences. Both were extremely well received. Hope Alliance is a church committed to reaching its Jerusalem, but also the ends of the earth.

Above all, Hope Alliance is committed to leadership development. The church has attracted an unusual number of strong leaders. While still a congregation of less than 100, it added two part-time staff members. One is a youth pastor, a radio announcer for a Christian station. The other is a self-employed businessman who serves as outreach pastor. He and his wife have moved into the small house on the church property. Four other men in the church are considering a ministry vocation.

Twelve leaders at Hope Alliance recently attended the "Growing a Healthy Church" seminar. The church is determined to make a difference in Cleveland. Part of its commitment includes planting daughter churches in nearby areas. Regardless of the sacrifice, Hope Alliance Bible Church is determined to be a healthy, Great Commission church.

Voices from the Past

I See a Great Need

Q. *Mr. Schenk, exactly what does that title mean, "Director of Extension"?*

A. Extension, as we use the term, refers to the founding of new churches.

Q. *How much need do you see for church extension in North America?*

A. I see a great need. In a recent article in *Christianity Today* Peter Wagner wrote that "more than 106 million American adults fall into the 'functionally unchurched' category." This is 74 percent. In other words, three out of every four American adults are lost and need to be evangelized.

Q. *Just how does one go about "planting" a new church?*

A. There are two ways, basically. Where there is a strong church in a given area, some members may, by reason of distance, decide they would like to start a new fellowship in the area where they live. With the support and assistance of the "mother" church, they begin a Bible class. As the new fellowship develops, the members think in terms of a community church.

Q. *You suggested that there is a second way to start churches?*

A. The other method is pioneering—going into an entirely new, unchurched area and beginning without a nucleus of people. This kind of church expansion requires particularly gifted leaders. It is difficult work.

Q. *What skills must an extension pastor have if he is to succeed?*

A. First, he needs the gift of evangelism. We are not out to proselyte from other churches, but to plant new churches with the specific goal of reaching unsaved people with the gospel of Jesus Christ. So the extension pastor must be gifted in winning people to Christ.

Q. *What kind of a record in church planting have you inherited as you take up this new responsibility?*

A. Actually quite a commendable one. From 1967 through 1975, 419 churches were opened. We experienced a normal attrition of church mergers and closures, leaving a net gain of 259.

Q. *Is it accurate to say that church extension offers some by-products besides simply the evangelizing of North America, as essential as that objective is?*

A. Very definitely. For one thing, it makes a wider base of support for our foreign missions. In five years a new church usually returns, through its contributions to the General Fund, as much money as the C&MA invested in it. One unusual success story is of a church that has returned to home and foreign missions over ten times our investment of $3,600—in only forty months.

Q. *Is there anything else you want to say?*

A. Yes, I wish that every person in our Alliance churches would become extension conscious and consider how he or she might become involved in church extension and local church growth. It might mean giving time to travel some miles to conduct Bible studies in another city. It might even mean taking temporary leadership in a new area where there is no Alliance church and carrying the heavy responsibility of seeing that a church is started.

An interview with the new
Director of Extension, Rev.
Raymond W. Schenk, Jr.,
The Alliance Witness,
February 7, 1977

Lessons from a Church Planter

by F. Mike Grubbs

It wasn't my intention to plant churches—here. I had it in my heart to do my church planting overseas, as an Alliance missionary. In fact, Carol and I, with our two children, Frank, four, and Charissa, one, had gone to the Alliance General Council in Lincoln, Nebraska, specifically to talk with officials in the Division of Overseas Ministries.

It had been a frustrating, disappointing experience. We had three strikes against us: age (too much), education (not enough) and a one-year-old daughter with severe asthma. I couldn't blame the men who turned us down. But why had God given us this heavy burden for missions and then denied us the opportunity to serve Him? It was maddening.

Guidance along the Interstate

Driving home, those thoughts were replaying

in my mind as I approached Columbus, Ohio, in the middle of the night. All my passengers were sound asleep. Suddenly, on one of the big green road signs along the interstate, God showed me a vision. Superimposed on that road sign were the faces of people.

It startled me. Thinking I must be really tired, I blinked my eyes, rolled down the window and took a long draught of coffee. Two miles further down the interstate, another sign came into view. There were the faces again! Only this time flames seemed to be consuming them and they looked to be in agony.

I couldn't take any more. I stopped the car, got out and sat on the guiderail in the glare of my headlights. And in that spot along the interstate, in the middle of the night, God gave me a three-word message: "Plant My Church!"

I had no idea what this meant, but my heart rejoiced. I was ecstatic! God had not abandoned me after all. There was something He wanted me to do that evidently He thought I could do!

Actually, I have been involved in three church plantings: two in Ohio, the third in Bedminster, New Jersey. (I will say more about Bedminster a little later.) All were accomplished with the help of a "mother" (sponsoring) church.

I discovered that consistent things happen in these endeavors. You start a home Bible study. As the word gets around that you are hoping to plant a new church, you can count on several types of people showing up. They form almost a pattern—like successive ocean waves rolling toward the shore. How you handle each of the "waves" spells the success or failure of your endeavor.

The Hard-working, Loyal Core

Every church planting needs a generous supply of core people. The more, the better! They desire to see the gathering succeed. They want to bring glory to God and spiritual growth to each member. They will be faithful in prayer and love and perseverance.

. A caveat: Everyone who is charter is not core! Your core group, by and large, will remain faithful to the vision. They do not wash over the bow and disappear. They stay with you. And they are an invaluable asset.

The Hurting and Damaged

You can expect some of the hurting and damaged. Usually they have been pushed out of other churches. It may be for any of a thousand reasons. Sometimes it is because of personality, behavior or attitude. Or maybe they just landed in a hornet's nest and got stung.

They come with a feeling of rejection. They are in need of deep healing and a loving community of very strong believers. They need the fellowship of people who know Jesus intensely and can communicate His love. They need people who are long-suffering with the unlovely.

If this wave is too high, it can swamp the ship. The acute needs of this group can move the focus of the study from outreach to healing. They may steal the evangelistic zeal and fervor of the group, replacing it with a pall of hopelessness and despair.

If not too many and of the right character, this wave can enhance a group. If too large and the leadership not mature enough, they can destroy the vision.

The Disillusioned, Angry, Aggressive

At face value, this wave may look no different from the hurting and damaged. But they are. In a sense, they share the rejection, frustration and despair of the hurting and damaged, but they do not wallow in self-pity. They have learned to blame, project, reproach and denounce those who have rejected them. People like this make it difficult to maintain a positive focus and an attitude of love and good will.

The venom of this group borders on hatred. Slander and malice are often the tools of their trade. Often they can see no good whatsoever in the churches from which they departed. Their hurt and anger colors every thought and word. One can hope that the love of Jesus, evidenced in the faithful, will bring repentance and healing. But if this type is too numerous, or if the leaders are unequipped to handle them, they can devastate the group.

The "Hypers"

In a new church planting, even before the term *church* is used, leaders are struggling to define and communicate its shape and form. The "hypers" who show up are powerful, spiritually immature and sometimes a force for evil. They want to define the new church.

"Hypers" are particularly dangerous at the beginning, and they are many. There are hyper-dispensationalists, hyper-Calvinists, hyper-Arminians, hyper-charismatics. There are hyper-legalists and hyper-liberationists.

They specialize in their field of study. That is what gives them distinction. These are people out of balance. Like an out-of-balance tire on an automobile, they can affect the whole ride, the whole church planting. These hypers tend to dominate discussions and filter everything through their particular grid. Because they are usually vocal, they may determine the public's perception of the group.

And the group begins to think, not in terms of balanced biblical Christianity, but in terms of this one-dimensional mind-set. The leader finds himself always trying to balance the group without offending the hypers. If a leader begins to answer questions from a defensive posture, he should beware. It's an indication that the hyperism already is shaping the group's identity.

The Seekers

This wave we all pray for and hope for! It is comprised of all sorts of people in all walks of life with all kinds of stories. But they have one commonality: they need the Savior. They are hungering and thirsting for something and Someone larger than themselves. Although they may not be able to articulate it, they are desperate for Jesus!

They are a joy to watch as the Savior is revealed through Scripture, prayer, song, testimony and teaching. This wave is not without its problems (after all, they are breathing!). But any church planter counts it a high privilege to work with seekers.

Seekers need a solid core of mature Christians willing to disciple and grow with them. But give them that and they will catch the vision. They will provide the future leadership for the church the planting pastor envisions!

It Can Be Done

Church planting done in step with Jesus works. In eleven years the church at Bedminster grew to 245 people, not all of them formal members. We purchased a property for $800,000 (New Jersey is an area of high prices!). We made renovations totaling another

$250,000—all of it debt free!

We built Grace Fellowship on "relational ministry"—people ministering to each other in small groups. Home Fellowship Groups (HFGs), we called them. HFGs kept the staff to a minimum. Besides, members learned to use the spiritual gifts God gave them to build the church body. Through this "one anothering," most of the ministry was accomplished.

Was everyone well loved and cared for? No. As with any experience, people made mistakes and people were hurt. That is why we have confession of sin and repentance!

But today Grace Fellowship is a very loving community. Its members are a tremendously giving people. I thank God for allowing Carol and me the privilege of working with Him in church planting.

Let's Build a Stronger Base

Have you spent any time recently in prayerful concern for the future of The Christian and Missionary Alliance? As our Society comes nearer the end of its first century of world ministry, we must give much more serious consideration to the extension of the home base, for this ultimately determines the measure of our work overseas.

After eighty-two years as a missionary society, the Alliance ranks eighth among Protestant groups in the number of overseas missionaries. Our missionary work abroad has been so spectacular that many think of us only as a missionary board, overlooking the more than 1,300 Alliance congregations which have faithfully grown and matured and ministered as the home base of this missionary alliance known around the globe.

Throughout North America these Alliance congregations in their daily witness and outreach underscore the fact that we must share the good news of Jesus Christ with millions here at home while we forward the ministry of our workers overseas.

Although Dr. A.B. Simpson and his fellow founders of the Alliance did not plan to establish another homeland denomination, they soon realized that any significant work abroad called for a corresponding endeavor at home. Plainly the urgent spiritual needs of the North American continent never captivated the imagination and enthusiasm of the Alliance family as did the foreign work. There was a commonly held philosophy which insisted that "if we will care for the work abroad, God will care for the work at home." While we built our great bridges to the twenty-four mission fields, we failed to span the lesser distances to needy people in the homeland.

Today greater numbers of our pastors and laymen believe that the time has come for us to embark on an imaginative, evangelistic program of extending Christ's ministry through our churches and witness in North America.

There are urgent reasons for a strong new thrust. First, the spiritual condition in North America and our mandate to preach the gospel everywhere demand action. The "all the world" of the Great Commission does not exclude North America. The Alliance must give serious attention to the needs of the home base where the spiritual situation becomes more desperate by the day. We cannot go on under the delusion that all is well. We must take more seriously our responsibility to evangelize the indifferent, unevangelized people of our own continent.

Second, it is impossible for us to continue our expansion abroad without developing a significantly stronger base from which to work. The witness overseas cannot long remain bright if the work at home lacks strength and vitality. Throughout the past four decades of Alliance history only meager sums of money have been available for the development of our work in North America. The 1969 budget of the Home Department, 10 percent of the General Fund, could designate only $160,000 for home field development. How many churches can we expect to add to our roster with this amount? The total for all the work of development at home is pitifully small and very inadequate.

Not only must churches be started, but they must have aid until they can carry their own responsibilities.

The 1970s have been designated as "The Decade of Development" for our home work. Plans call for a massive effort. The "other cities" of North America need our message, our witness. The opportunities are so numerous that all currently available funds could be spent in a single district or a single metropolitan area.

What is the answer? First and foremost, there must be men for these extension efforts. We rejoice in the increased number of men who are responding. An accompanying need is adequate finances. Congregations must be helped as they build houses of worship in areas new to the Alliance. Here is opportunity to help penetrate untouched areas of our continent. This is not just another in a series of appeals. We ask you to give it the highest priority.

—Rev. L.W. Pippert,
The Alliance Witness,
December 10, 1969

	A Vision to
CHAPTER	Reach Out
17	
	by Edna Mapstone

When Korean-born Samuel Sung Lee graduated from Alliance Theological Seminary, he could not see beyond his fellow Koreans. Not that he held prejudices against other races. But the large number of Koreans in major American cities—New York, Los Angeles, Chicago—constituted sufficient challenge.

If Samuel Lee had been thinking beyond Koreans, he might have guessed that God had bigger plans. When God called him to the ministry, He impressed on Samuel Lee the words of Proverbs 3:5-6:

> Trust in the LORD with all your heart
> and lean not on your own understanding;
> in all your ways acknowledge him,
> and he will make your paths straight.

A Transforming Missions Trip

All through his seminary years, Samuel

served in ministries involving exclusively Koreans. Graduating with a degree in urban ministries, he became associate pastor of a Korean church in Los Angeles. But God was about to do a new thing in Samuel Lee's life.

Pastor Lee's main responsibility in the Los Angeles church was to second-generation Korean youth. One youth project that Samuel devised was a missions trip to Africa.

There in Africa with a group of his young people, Samuel Lee suddenly realized something. God's love is not restricted to any particular race. God loves *all* people. Samuel returned to Los Angeles thoroughly excited about the dimensions of this new-to-him concept. Los Angeles, as much as any other American city, was multiracial. Where better to evangelize the "nations"?

Samuel discussed his vision with the church's senior pastor, a man he looked to as a mentor and friend. To his joy, he discovered the senior pastor shared his desire to reach out to other ethnic groups within the city. Together they spent many hours planning how to go about such an evangelistic outreach.

An Overwhelming Disappointment

But it was not to be—at least, there, and at that time. The senior pastor unexpectedly died. His death was a shattering blow to Samuel Lee. When the church elders decided to take the church in other directions, Samuel resigned, thoroughly disillusioned.

The Alliance Korean District learned of Samuel's availability. Although the Los Angeles church was not Alliance, the Korean District had ordained Samuel to the ministry, and they needed someone of his qualifications to be associate pastor at South West Korean Alliance Church in Palos Hills, South Chicago. Specifically, they needed someone to be pastor to about twenty English-speaking Koreans who met in a classroom of the church.

Samuel Lee explained to the church that he was still recovering emotionally from the Los Angeles trauma. He had no real heart to enter into another ministry yet. The church understood and accepted him anyhow. The year was 1990.

Despite the pall that he could not quite shake off, God blessed his ministry in Palos Hills. The congregation of twenty soon became a congregation of fifty. It was all Pastor Lee could do to keep up with the influx of newcomers. And not all were Koreans. It was an ethnic mix. Slowly the vision of a multi-ethnic evangelistic ministry, eclipsed in Los Angeles, reappeared to Samuel in Chicago!

Found in the Yellow Pages

One day a Filipino family found the church through the yellow pages. This family belonged to a Bible study group that was looking for a church. Soon other members of the group began to attend.

This was, Pastor Lee admits, "quite interesting," since he had never had a Filipino friend in his life. The sudden influx of Filipinos took the Korean congregation by surprise. And before long, some Chinese families also began to attend. Soon the newcomers—Filipinos and Chinese—outnumbered the Koreans!

Seeing what God was doing, the Korean senior pastor acted with commendable wisdom. He realized that the two congregations could best grow as separate churches: A Korean-language church to minister to the many Koreans in South Chicago. And a multi-ethnic, English language church to meet the needs of those in that category. Sensing God's timing in this development, Samuel Lee offered to go with the new group as their pastor.

Fortuitously, the Alliance had a Caucasian congregation in Westmont: Westmont Alliance Church. This church, led by Rev. Warren Gentry, opened its doors to the new congregation, allowing them to meet in its building. The first Sunday of April 1992 marked the beginning.

It was an exciting start but filled with uncertainties too. God had anticipated it all, and from the start He had prepared people to join this beginning group. Slowly but steadily the church grew.

Faith Alliance Bible Church, the name of the new planting, did not depend on its Sunday meetings for all the action. In due course of time, they had established twelve home Bible studies. Pastor Lee found himself teaching "almost every day, moving from one Bible study to another."

What Next?

All was well and good. But where should the church go from that point? They decided to invite Rev. Gerald R. Mapstone, superintendent of the Midwest District, for a two-day leadership training seminar.

Mr. Mapstone's first question at the seminar was "What is your vision for this church?" An embarrassed Pastor Lee admitted that they did not have a vision except to hold as many home Bible studies as possible. His real focus, he said, was on keeping up with all the new people and leading the Bible studies.

With the guidance of the superintendent, the church leaders spent most of the two days formulating a mission statement. As they pondered the matter and waited upon God, the leaders came up with five points:

1. *To establish care groups*. These would be not simply Bible studies but an effort to see that all the congregation was involved in small-group, one-another ministry.

2. *To have their own building in five years*. Despite the generosity of Westmont Alliance Church, Faith Alliance Bible Church needed a permanent home of its own in the community.

3. *To support overseas Alliance missions.* They were in a denomination whose middle name was "Missionary"! They needed to be a significant player in this goal of reaching all nations with the gospel.

4. *To pursue evangelism and outreach at home.* A needy city lay all around them. They were a part of God's plan to bring it under the sound and power of the gospel.

5. *To develop and support full-time church workers.* Both the development and the support were critical. They needed to seek out and train these potential men and women. They needed to support financially and in other ways those who would be serving their church.

Deciding exactly what Faith Alliance Bible Church should be doing was the medicine it needed. At last the leaders had some concrete objectives to aim for. With those objectives in place, both the leaders and the congregation were ready to move forward.

Faith Alliance Clones Itself

Back in 1992, when Faith Alliance Bible Church began, the leaders had made a promise to God. As soon as the congregation reached 120 people, they would plant a new church. None of them supposed the time would come so quickly! In less than three years they were at the predetermined attendance level. In keeping with their promise, they began looking for a location.

It was the Lord's timing—the leaders are sure of it. Their search coincided with the availability of property in Des Plaines on the north side of Chicago. The new church opened in Des Plaines in September 1995. Already the diverse ethnic congregation has increased to 150! The worshipers fill the sanctuary to capacity, making expansion a necessity.

And what is the name of this new church? Faith Alliance Bible Church—just like the parent congregation! One is in Westmont, the other is in Des Plaines.

But the exciting story does not stop there. The leaders of these two churches wanted to evangelize college students by establishing Bible studies on the campuses. Pastor Lee started with two students at the University of Illinois at Chicago. Now he is ministering to over 100 students who meet Wednesdays as one large group and other days in smaller groups. At Northern Illinois College, twenty-five additional students meet Monday evenings for Bible study.

Are More Surprises in Store?

Sometimes Pastor Lee reflects back on his Koreans-only goal as he completed his seminary work. He is grateful his own plans did not pan out. God had bigger and better plans in store for him.

If you should ask Samuel Lee about the future, he probably will hesitate. He knows from experience that God's plans turn out to be bigger than anything he imagines! He hopes God will continue to surprise him.

Already, it is an enviable record. Two healthy, reproducing churches. Two exciting Bible study groups on college campuses. God has been in it—obviously. And Samuel Lee has had solid, dedicated help from those associated with him. Still, it goes to show what God can do when a person is willing to obey Him.

In a sense, Pastor Lee and his leadership teams are not *working* at winning people and planting churches. Rather, they are naturally *living out* what is within them—a dynamic relationship with Jesus Christ.

Isn't that what church planting is all about?

Voices from the Past

Opening New Churches

There are more church members (over 100 million) in the United States than ever before. . . . But are we really meeting the need?

Solomon has told us that "for everything there is . . . a time. . . . A time to be born, and a time to die; a time to plant, and a time to pluck up that which is planted." In God's historical plan for the ages, present-day religious trends seem to indicate that today, more than ever before, is a time to plant.

God is calling churchmen and lay Christians today to the task of planting—not a botanical, but a spiritual organism. The fertile soil is a new frontier, one vastly more productive than the Post-Reformation European terrain.

The world is dying for a little bit of love. A genuine passion for souls will cause us to seek ways of reaching those for whom Christ died. Christ put His hand upon people as he visited them in their homes; so must His present-day disciples. *We must go to the people.* We cannot wait for them to come to us. As we go to these new areas, we are taking the church to the people.

The greatest point in favor [of planting churches] is that it opens the door to personal soul-winning. This great door and effectual is now opened unto you.

We too must "move out" for God. If we do not we may be "left out" in the end.

—Rev. Kenneth Paul Berg,
Ph.D., *The Alliance Weekly*,
November 7, 1956

A Church for Our Capital

by David Wong

It was unheard of. The 1990 General Council of The Christian and Missionary Alliance was held in Washington, DC, yet at that time the Alliance had neither presence nor witness in all the District of Columbia.

As founding pastor of Chinese Alliance Church in nearby Gaithersburg, Maryland, I sensed God's nudge. Perhaps he wanted me to consider starting a church in this internationally important urban center.

My wife, Nancy, and I talked over the ramifications. We also discussed the possibility with our children, Melodie and Jordan. We found them very supportive. Our personal research led us to believe we needed to target another "Unreached People Group"—the international community.

The Alliance Mid-Atlantic District invested in a demographic study that confirmed our findings. The move from vision to venture took a year. Meanwhile, we shared our hopes with two other couples. And in a short time, God had added still others to our core group.

Going against Accepted Theory

A church targeting internationals runs counter to the church growth principle of homogeneous groups. The accepted wisdom is that people want to worship with people most nearly like themselves. Koreans with Koreans. Xers with Xers. Blue-collar with blue-collar. And we were hoping to plant a church of people from various ethnic, linguistic and cultural backgrounds.

It might be contrary to church growth theory, but it was in sync with the Bible mandate to reach all peoples. We wanted to equip believers to be ambassadors of Christ charged with the ministry of reconciliation.

We announced our first worship service for September 8, 1991. Our venue would be the Holiday Inn on Wisconsin Avenue. It was in the diverse and upscale Georgetown area of Washington. To that first service more than a hundred people came!

Statistical data indicate that forty-eight percent of the people moving into Washington are singles. One-fifth of the newcomers are from a foreign country. Clearly we had a large segment of people to work with!

In the weeks and months that followed, the Lord brought to the church people who could support its work. He brought people who lived near the Holiday Inn willing to open their homes for weekly Bible studies and prayer meetings. Others involved themselves in teaching children and conducting children's church. A quality sound system was provided at no expense to the church.

Reaping the Ripened Harvest

More importantly, the Lord brought seekers. A businesswoman from Brazil, a guest at the hotel, came to the worship service. At the closing invitation she received Jesus Christ as her Savior! A number of Chinese scholars attending one of our church-sponsored Bible studies have made Jesus their Lord. More than twenty have been baptized, including a few who by now have returned to China.

To date, people from eighty-four countries and territories have joined in worship with this unique, multinational congregation. The mix includes diplomats, visiting foreign government officials, local politicians, students from Georgetown University and young professionals. They are a reflection of the church's mission: *To be a dynamic congregation relating to one another in all their diversity, joining together to impact Washington with the reality and relevancy of Jesus.*

Many have been drawn in by the caring ministries of the church. The congregation is friendly. They do not hesitate to invite their friends to the services. Internationals commonly turn to the movie theaters for their entertainment, so to attract them to our church, I often title my sermons after a hit movie.

Challenges, Innovations

Many challenges have surfaced to test Washington International Church. Government cutbacks and corporate job transfers keep the church composition in a state of constant flux. High real estate costs have thus far deprived us of a building of our own.

But the members rise to each challenge. We are now meeting at St. Luke's United Methodist Church, right below the Russian embassy. This move has allowed the church to have a more effective witness and exposure to the community. The larger facilities have allowed us to expend our outreach ministries.

One of those outreaches is our World Class Language Institute. It offers tuition-free conversational English classes. We do not lack for people anxious to improve their English. In meeting that need we have opportunity, as well, to share the gospel of Jesus Christ. Church members donate money and time to make this effort successful.

We also sponsor a monthly Saturday night coffee house. Gourmet coffee, exotic food and wholesome entertainment—all free—emphasize in creative ways the gospel of God's free grace. On average 125 people attend. Some of them show up at church the next morning. A few have found the Lord.

A prominent Washington law firm donated thirty computers to the church for a computer training center. This ties in with other in-the-planning ministries of the church. These include a career development center, a health and legal referral clinic and a "business incubator" for micro enterprises. Today's urban ministry calls for a demonstration of social responsibility. In that context, Christians can show their faith by their actions.

Bearing Children Too

Washington International Church intends to have "daughter" churches. The Chinese Bible study, mentioned above, has now been organized as a church of forty people. It is reaching out to those who come from the People's Republic of China. A fellowship of Hispanics is in the nurturing stage. Our expectation, a few years from now, is an Alliance Spanish-speaking church in the District of Columbia. We hope to apply the same strategy with other language groups.

Drawing upon the strength of its cultural diversity, the church continues to be a beacon in a dark place. Our people believe this unique ministry is on the cutting edge of church planting. In time, *every* denomination will be intentionally targeting internationals in their church planting efforts.

The world has come to America's doorstep. We must tell these visitors, students and immigrants about God's love. We must help them find hope in such a time as this.

Voices from the Past

The Alliance Development Fund: A "Family" Project

It's a joy to have a part in the establishing of new Alliance churches," comments a member of the Alliance family in Washington State. "God bless the work of our Society everywhere."

"We are more than glad to make this investment with The Christian and Missionary Alliance," writes an Alliance member in Michigan. "We know it will be used to further the cause of Christ in this fair land of ours."

Blanchard Road Alliance Church in Wheaton, Illinois, is a good example of how funds are put to good use as God's people let their savings work for church growth.

In 1974 Blanchard Road Alliance had an average attendance of 104. The next year the church borrowed from the Church Extension Loan Fund in order to erect a new church building. The assistance enabled them to move out of a Masonic temple into their own facilities.

By 1977 average attendance had doubled to 212. So far this year attendance is averaging over 300. Pastor Ronald Gifford gives enthusiastic praise to God for the timely financial help his church has received.

The combination of concerned people willing to invest and dedicated workers eager to use these funds for church growth will certainly produce an increasing harvest for God's kingdom.

—Merlin C. Feather,
The Alliance Witness,
October 18, 1978

Preplanned Delivery

by David A. Toth

Two years before we put a pastor in West Chester, Ohio, I knew we should have an Alliance church there. What once had been corn fields along Interstate 75 northwest of Cincinnati was fast becoming Boom Town! New home construction dotted the landscape. Two brand-new elementary schools were already in place. Two new high schools were under construction.

These thousands of new people were productive, prosperous and, for the most part, pagan.

We—meaning all of us at the Ohio Valley District Office in Cincinnati—began praying. We prayed that we would find a man who was focused on establishing a conversion-oriented church. During a meeting of the District Development Committee, we drove out I-75 to the West Chester exit. By the side of the road we prayed that God would provide us an Alliance church in West Chester. We prayed particularly that He would send us the pastor of His choosing.

The Pieces Fall into Place

God answered prayer in the person of Tim Huckins. Tim and his wife, Teri, with the experience of several pastorates behind them, wanted to "pioneer." In our district we have a thorough assessment process for church planters. Both Tim and Teri earned high marks. We have not been disappointed. Both are "people" persons. It has been clear from the start that God gifted them for church planting.

We did much advance planning even before Tim Huckins and his family moved on site. Purposely, we had made no prior contacts there. My desire was that the man selected by God should be the unchallenged vision-bearer and leader. But we planned thoroughly, even to setting a tentative date for the first service.

Tim and Teri moved to West Chester in September 1996. At once they began making contacts and developing relationships. Tim made a number of friends playing basketball at the Y, and Teri developed contacts through their children's activities at the Y and in school. (At the district office, we have never doubted our decision to provide Tim and Teri with a family membership to the Y. It has paid for itself many times over!)

By Christmas 1996, three couples had committed themselves to be part of the church's core group. In March, Tim and Teri held an "interested persons meeting." The turnout was less than expected, but those who came were enthusiasts. Suddenly the core group jumped in size to about forty people!

Evangelism and Leadership Development

Tim's focus during this gestation period was evangelism and leadership development. He—and we—knew that he must model an evangelistic lifestyle and work to develop leaders. Followers are everywhere. If you can develop leaders, the followers will follow!

By summer 1997, the core group numbered about fifty and two cell groups were meeting regularly. Near the end of the summer, a third cell group was added. It was time to get ready for "Birth Sunday."

Tim and Teri were working hard to equip their core people for the various necessary ministries. For West Chester, we saw these "systems" as four: worship, children, youth and small groups. Only with these systems in place could we say with integrity that we were ready to minister in West Chester.

We held two "practice" services, one on September 14 and one on September 21. During that time we identified and addressed the "bugs" and gave everyone last-minute instructions.

A wonderful sense of expectancy came over the core group as it anticipated "Birth Sunday,"

September 28. That expectancy continues to this day!

But we had one more major step. We called it Super Saturday. On September 27 some thirty-one churches sent representatives. People came from six denominations and from five states. Two by two, they canvassed more than 2,500 West Chester homes with brochures and invitations. The canvassers had 300 opportunities to present the gospel, and some fifty people prayed to receive Christ!

Super Saturday positioned us for a tremendous Birth Sunday!

Birth Sunday Arrives

At 10 o'clock Sunday, September 28, 152 people joined together for the birth of Cedarbrook Community Church. The superintendent of Lakota School District was on hand to welcome the group. The superintendent of the Ohio Valley District, Dr. David F. Presher, shared words of encouragement.

After an enthusiastic time of singing, led by a praise ensemble, Pastor Tim preached a message from God's Word. The whole day was tremendously uplifting and inspiring. The church had a healthy birth!

During October, Sunday attendance leveled back to about 100. The church launched a fourth cell group. At age three weeks, Cedarbrook hosted its first missionary conference. The Great Commission faith promise commitment totaled more than $7,000! Without question, the "DNA" of Cedarbrook is evangelistic and outward focused! It is already planning to birth a daughter church in the next few years.

By the grace of God and the power of the Holy Spirit, Cedarbrook Community Church will impact West Chester and the world!

Voices from the Past

Global Expansion

Within weeks The Christian and Missionary Alliance intends to launch an eight-year program of global expansion that will challenge the spiritual resources of all its people.

The goal is to double by 1987—the C&MA's centenary. At first calculation it seems ridiculously easy. If every two members and adherents in the next eight years won just three people to Christ—and to the church—the goal would be in hand, even allowing for natural attrition through deaths and other causes. But the fact is that never has the C&MA—or any other church of substantial size—doubled itself in so short a time. The goal challenges the very utmost of every North American member.

There will be some who feel that goal-setting is basically unspiritual and should not be countenanced. They argue that God is sovereign, that we are to be workers with Him and that the "increase" is His to determine.

We are quick to acknowledge that it is God who gives the increase, but we respectfully beg to disagree that therefore we have no right to ask God in faith for definite numbers. When Jesus commanded His followers to "ask, . . .

that your joy may be full" (John 16:24). He set no limitations. Certainly the prayer that He will add 192,000 more members to His church is pleasing to a God who is "not willing that any should perish, but that all should come to repentance" (2 Peter 3:9).

In short, to hope to double our size so that we can boast of our achievement is carnal and inappropriate; to hope to double our size for the sake of perishing people and an ever more effective worldwide ministry is spiritual and worthy.

As Dr. King said in announcing the Board-approved guidelines, "This global expansion must begin with a new sense of personal dedication by each officer, each pastor and missionary, each member and adherent. It is only possible as we unitedly recognize that it will come 'not by might nor by power, but by [God's] Spirit.' "

—Editorial,
The Alliance Witness,
February 7, 1979

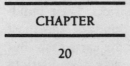

Church Planting on a Shoestring

by Vergil G. Schmidt

From the beginning, God has been in the planting of Fellowship Community Church in Midland, Texas. I say that as I look back on the church's three-year existence.

For my wife, Raychel, and me, our involvement goes back beyond May 1995, when Fellowship Community Church formally began. In fact, for my wife, *considerably* farther back. This mid-Texas city of 100,000 people is home to her! On our vacation trips to Midland from our ministries in Alberta, Canada, we had a growing sense of God's call to plant an Alliance church in Midland.

On one such trip we happened to be driving around the city and saw the new Abel Junior High School, Midland's pride and joy. On impulse we stopped and took a tour of the building. Once inside, I could visualize a church meeting in those beautiful facilities. Some two years later, what I visualized was reality!

"The Good Lord Was Watchin' out for You!"

Renting space to church congregations is routine for most school districts. Their buildings are otherwise idle on Sundays, and most school districts are glad for the extra cash. But Abel Junior High School was the district's showpiece. Until *we* asked, the answer had always been, "No."

Even the custodian expressed surprise.

"How did you get this place?" he wanted to know. I told him we had simply made application and the board had approved our request.

"The good Lord was watchin' out for you!" was his comment. We certainly agreed.

But it takes more than a building—even a showplace building like Abel Junior High—to make a church. This planting began well ahead of May 1995, when we held our first service.

As I said, God's call to us was a growing conviction. On one of our trips to Midland, we had circled by the Southwestern District office in Fort Worth. We talked with Rev. Louis T. Dechert, at the time director of extension for the district. He was enthusiastic about having an Alliance church in Midland. But funds for extension were already stretched thin. We probably should not count on very much financial support from the Southwest District.

We were convinced that Midland was God's

call, and His call would entail His provision. By the time Raychel and I moved to Midland to begin church planting, we had the promise of about $15,000. That much to pay rent, support our family, cover advertising and do all the other things necessary to plant a church. And do it until the church could meet its own budget. (To God's glory, I report that in just nine months the church was able to be free of all subsidy.)

A Very Modest Beginning

Nine adults and three children constituted our core group—the majority of them members of Raychel's family. Until then, none of the nine had had connections with The Christian and Missionary Alliance. Meeting regularly with them, I began several months of teaching and training. Each meeting strengthened the bond between members of the group and brought new reality to our church-planting vision.

As the pastor, I have attempted to pattern this church after the "Meta Church" concept. In essence, that is to train and equip lay people to do the work of ministry through relationship-building. As the members grasped the principles, they reached out to relatives, neighbors and other associates. Eventually, our first "cell" divided into two.

One man, a member of the original group, really began to grow. He looked forward to each of these Sunday meetings. This was out of character for him. Up to this point he had been a "loner," not enjoying the company of others. He grew to where he willingly shared his testimony publicly at our organizational meeting and Christmas banquet. He now serves as one of our lay pastors. He and his wife lead a cell whose primary purpose is community evangelism. Together they have a great ministry within our church.

Thirteen Converts—and Counting

Nothing is quite as exciting as witnessing a person's new birth as he or she comes to know Jesus Christ personally. Thus far, the Lord has given us thirteen new converts. I wish the number was several times higher, but we are profoundly thankful for these thirteen. Most of them have come as our members reached out to family and friends.

One of them, however, simply showed up at a Sunday morning worship service. At the conclusion she requested us to pray for her healing. Before the elders anointed her with oil and prayed (James 5:14-15), I asked if she knew Jesus Christ personally.

"No, I don't," she responded, "but I would like to." That was all any of us needed to hear! We led her in the prayer of faith and she became a believer. I wish I could report her physical healing. For whatever reason, God chose not to answer our prayers for that need.

Barring divine intervention, she hasn't long to live. But she is bound for a land much better than this one.

An AWANA Club

Another fruitful aspect of our Midland ministry has been our AWANA Club for school-age children through sixth grade. The AWANA "commander" took the assignment with no previous ministry experience except as driver of the church bus. Though it began with eighteen children, the program today sees nearly fifty on a typical Wednesday evening. And it continues to grow. We are planning to develop a Junior Varsity Club to reach teenagers.

It has been heartening to observe the AWANA commander's personal growth. Before his commitment to AWANA, he had never spoken in public. Now, on occasion at club meetings, he teaches the Bible lesson to the children. He also promotes AWANA publicly before much larger adult audiences. He will tell you he is grateful that God brought him to Fellowship Community Church. There he has developed leadership skills he never knew he had!

Healing for the Emotionally Hurting

A number of our Fellowship Community Church people have come out of churches that exercised undue control over their members. Hurt emotionally by their bad experiences elsewhere, they now are trying to recover. One of these commented that almost everyone at Fellowship Community appears to be struggling with some painful experience. The observation is true. I hope we will never lose sight of the fact that we minister to a world that is hurting.

It's hard to find anyone who is not carrying some kind of a pain or heavy burden. As a church fellowship, we are purposefully trying to be Jesus' outstretched hands to such people. We choose to be a hospital for sinners, not a playground for saints.

"When We Asunder Part"

Because Midland is an oil town, there is considerable congregational turnover due to job transfers. We have lost a number of people who had been assimilated into our church's ministry life. These have had as difficult a time leaving our church as the rest of us have had letting them go. I have remained in contact with everyone. Without exception, they tell me how much they miss being in our fellowship.

What they miss the most, they say, is the time we devoted to relationship-building. Some of those who left have used their experience at Fellowship Community as a standard for choosing a church in their new location. But not always can they find a church that approximates this one. Those who cannot have struggled considerably, wishing only to be back in Midland!

This is not to suggest that no other churches are having a ministry equal to ours. That simply is not true. But for those God brought into our fellowship, the bearing of one another's burdens was an important step in their spiritual growth. We remain grateful to God for the privilege of having ministered to them for as long as they were with us.

A Missionary Vision

Because The Christian and Missionary Alliance is a missionary denomination, we have found it a joy to share that vision. Many of our members had never before been part of such a global outreach.

The Lord brought one member into our fellowship who previously had been involved with Precept Ministries. He had been to the Ukraine more than once. God used him and used our missionary conferences to challenge and invigorate people to personalize missions. Now missions is a part of their lifestyle.

As a result of this missionary emphasis, three of our men are planning an overseas missions trip in the near future. And more and more of our people are supporting the Alliance's Great Commission Fund.

It is a rare privilege, as a new local church, to host the founding meeting of a new missions outreach. Fellowship Community Church has had that privilege. We hosted the organizational meeting of the North American Committee for the Filipino International Network. This is an interdenominational missionary group founded to assist Filipinos around the world. It will supply them with needed resources to conduct Bible studies and build churches.

Fellowship Community Church is committed to being a force for God and righteousness not only locally but worldwide.

Voices from the Past

Get Ready for 100 New Churches

Never before has the U.S. Alliance attempted something so daring, so innovative or so large scale. The venture, called "Easter 100," could add a new dimension to the denomination's view of church planting and yield an evangelistic harvest of unprecedented proportions.

During a recent interview Rev. Paul Radford, national director of extension and overseer of the "Easter 100" project, offered his perspective on this nationwide plan.

Warren Bird: *What is the purpose of "Easter 100"?*

Paul Radford: We hope to reach unsaved, unchurched people with the gospel in at least 100 communities. Our geographical and ethnic districts will start 100 new churches or more, each of which will hold its first public worship service on Easter Sunday 1987 (April 19).

W.B.: *Where did the 100-church goal come from?*

P.R.: Originally I had wanted to begin 20 churches using this planned strategy. But, at the Louisville Council in 1985, Rev. Francis McGeaughay, Rev. Richard Bailey and I were talking about the idea. Francis stated,

"Anybody can start 20 churches. Let's ask God to stretch our faith to aim for 100!" Mr. Bailey added, "That would be great." And the matter was settled!

W.B.: *How exactly will these churches be started? And how will they differ from a typical, already existing C&MA congregation?*

P.R.: The "Easter 100" philosophy involves three distinctives. First, a targeted area is surveyed to determine certain community needs, and then the new church is structured to meet those needs. If people are concerned about the quality of child care, for instance, the new congregation will use a registered nurse—in uniform—to head up its nursery.

Secondly, a ministry team of committed Christians sends out a community-wide mailing. The content is geared specifically to the unchurched and the unsaved. It addresses objections that these groups commonly cite. If people complain about boring sermons and formal worship liturgies, for example, the letter will pledge that sermons will be relevant to today and that music will be refreshingly contemporary.

Third, the worship style is designed to be as intelligible as possible to the non-Christian. For example, instead of embarrassing the unchurched by asking them to find John 3:16 in their Bible, the "Easter 100" preacher provides pew Bibles and directs participants to a certain page number.

W.B.: *Why are you so excited about what God might do this Easter?*

P.R.: The Bible tells us that the local church is God's idea, not ours. Therefore, a strategy to develop Christ-centered churches throughout the United States will surely have His anointing, especially since these "Easter 100" churches will target the unchurched and the unsaved. I commend "Easter 100" to every reader's prayers—and personal participation.

—Rev. Paul Radford,
The Alliance Witness,
November 19, 1986

<table>
<tr><td>CHAPTER
21</td><td></td></tr>
</table>

| CHAPTER

21 | A New
Chinese
Church
Reports |

by John Keh-Jung Guu

In 1994, Rev. David and Sara King, Alliance missionaries to Hong Kong, were on home assignment in Fort Myers, Florida. They were facing a ministry transition. As they sought the Lord's will, a Chinese Alliance pastor in Tampa suggested they consider the many Chinese right around them in Southwest Florida. Why not start a Chinese church in the Fort Myers area?

David and Sara prayerfully accepted the challenge as God's directive. With support from the Alliance Southeastern District and the Chinese Association, they went to work.

First Alliance Church in Fort Myers allowed Chinese Alliance Church to use its facilities. Financial help from The Village Church at Shell Point allowed Rev. John and Esther Guu to be added to the team. John and Esther were the perfect complement. The Guus spoke Mandarin; the Kings, Cantonese. The Kings were often the seed-sowers; the Guus the harvesters.

Here John Guu tells about three of those "harvests."

Mr. C

In his 50s, Mr. C is a Chinese from Malaysia. He used to be very rich, very influential. Until the Malaysian government falsely accused him. He lost everything, ending up in Florida, where he found menial work in a Chinese restaurant.

He joined about twenty other Chinese restaurant workers in a crowded apartment where I held Friday night Bible studies.

Some of the more profane residents called me "Jesus." As I arrived this particular day, one of these called out, "Here comes Jesus! Don't preach to us. Preach to this guy, Mr. C. If anyone needs Jesus, he does!"

Just then Mr. C staggered forward, a glass of wine in hand. At once he started firing accusations at me, never giving me opportunity to reply. *Can I endure this?* I wondered. The mustiness of the room, the smell of wine and sweat and the torrent of angry words were nauseating.

I lived through it and returned. Again and again. After several months of this, Mr. C began to appreciate my "patience." The fact was, he never gave me *opportunity* to answer him!

One day, out of nowhere, Mr. C said he wanted to go to church with me. After that, he began attending church regularly.

Then he began borrowing books from our mobile church library—three or four a week. Soon he had read almost every book we had. He was becoming very knowledgeable about Christianity.

One Friday night at the Bible study, Mr. C was obviously upset, complaining and angry. Our Bible study was about Jesus calming the stormy sea with a simple command.

"There is no storm that Jesus cannot calm," I said. "Just ask Jesus with faith, and He will do it for you."

"But Jesus cannot help me this time," Mr. C objected. I found out that he was about to be fired from his job because he complained so much.

"Let's pray and trust this situation to Jesus," I suggested. I asked God to intervene. Then I asked Mr. C if he would let Jesus be his Lord and Savior. To my surprise, he was willing.

When next I saw Mr. C, he was bubbling over with joy. He hadn't been fired after all. Instead, the boss had given him a raise! "Thanks, Jesus!" he kept saying. "Thanks, Jesus!"

When Jesus entered his life, the worst guy in the restaurant became the best!

Mr. and Mrs. Y

S and B, a Chinese husband and wife, came to faith in Christ at Chinese Alliance Church. B's parents, Mr. and Mrs. Y, living in mainland

China, were planning to visit them. I encouraged B to try to win her parents to the Lord while they were here.

At the time we were holding a Friday night Bible study in our home. And, sure enough, B brought her parents. Mr. and Mrs. Y were physically present, but it was obvious they did not enjoy the meeting. I discovered that Mrs. Y was a staunch Buddhist. Only later did I learn that Mr. Y was a high-ranking official in the communist government.

It was not a brief visit, and as time went on, Mrs. Y became interested in the gospel. At first she tried to convince me that all religions are valid and lead to the true God. I countered by explaining that Jesus is God's very Son, not merely another religious leader. He had to die to be our Savior. I also shared my personal testimony.

B continued to pray for her mother. We lent her the *Jesus* video, and afterwards I asked Mrs. Y what she thought of it. She said she cried after watching it. "Jesus' death was so touching," she added.

I followed that up with more gospel literature. She read every book in our church library. And I made sure she heard the gospel in my Sunday preaching. Soon she became a Christian.

For Mr. Y, apathy changed to sympathy. But because of his high rank in the China government, he hesitated to make a public confession.

Not long before he returned to China, Mr. Y was praying with me. He cried and cried aloud to the Lord. He had given his whole life to helping the communists, he said. Now he realized it was all a lie and all in vain. He felt cheated. He wanted to follow Christ the rest of his life.

Mr. and Mrs. Y have returned to China. For the sake of their other children, who do not know Christ yet, Mr. Y remains a secret believer. When his children turn to Christ, he promises, then as a family they will give public testimony to their faith.

B reports that her parents are standing firm in the Lord and growing stronger in Him.

Mrs. W

Mrs. W is from Taiwan, where she was a devoted Buddhist. She performed the temple services and gave much money to the temple.

In time she emigrated from Taiwan to America, married and had a son. Though she refused to step into a church, she and her husband, C, sent their son to a Catholic school. But they refused to attend any of the school functions.

Until the accident. Mrs. W had a car accident during her second pregnancy. She was not at fault, but the police ticketed her. A bitter lawsuit followed. Still the strong Buddhist, she promised Buddha if he would help her win, she would give him her entire life.

She lost.

It was about that time that she got acquainted with some people from Chinese Alliance Church. With her faith in Buddha shattered, she started coming to our church. The more she heard of the gospel, the less faith she had in Buddha. But she was offended whenever we declared Jesus to be the *only* way to God.

We visited her faithfully. She always welcomed us, but she feigned disinterest whenever we talked about Jesus. On one of the visits, I sensed God's leading to extend an invitation to Mrs. W.

She was ready.

I warned her that to receive Jesus she would have to throw out all her idols and Buddhist charms. She was prepared to take those steps.

Behind the idols are evil spirits. She renounced them too in the name of Jesus. The spirits would not give up. Never in her life had they been so persistent. But her faith stood firm. How? I don't know. God did it!

Mrs. W continues to attend church regularly. Everywhere she goes, she has the good news of Jesus on her tongue. All other gods are false. She tells people not to be fooled by the evil spirits.

Her husband is now a believer too. They have made their Cape Coral home available for a Bible study.

From the founding of Chinese Alliance Church in Fort Myers, we have prayed to see one conversion a month. God has answered that prayer. And He continues to answer it!

Expert Discusses Alliance Church Growth

The C&MA set a goal to double its inclusive membership between 1978 and 1987. What is your perspective on that approach to church growth?

The Centennial Advance is the most significant denominational goal-setting project that has been implemented in America or Canada. I feel that the C&MA is setting a role model for others. It takes great boldness to project doubling over such a short period. Because Alliance leadership knows church growth principles and how to implement them, goal ownership has been widespread.

I am quite sure that by your 1987 centennial more men and women will be won to Christ and incorporated into a church than would have been if the goal had not been set. I doubt whether your "Easter 100" project would have been conceived without the pressure of knowing that new churches were needed to reach your doubling objective.

What is your opinion of this Alliance strategy for starting 100 new churches on Easter Sunday 1987?

It is one of the most creative visions I have encountered. Several important factors surfaced in the five pilot projects begun on Easter Sunday 1986. One is that a large percentage of the opening-day crowds were unchurched people. Another is that these churches cost an average of $10,000 each to start. That is a highly economical method when compared, for example, to another denomination which calculates a start-up cost of $500,000 per church! If these two things can be sustained, I think "Easter 100" has tremendous potential.

Any final words?

The Alliance faces the danger that after 1987 there can be a psychological letdown because people will tire of church growth and turn all their energies to maintenance and consolidation. That would be fatal. The momentum has been building for eight years. New goals need to be set. This era of Centennial Advance should be but a launch-pad for a second century of tremendous growth.

—C. Peter Wagner
(with Warren Bird),
The Alliance Witness,
July 30, 1986

	A Re-plant in
CHAPTER	**the Desert**
22	
	by Jim Corley

Rita Ranch Community Church, Tucson, Arizona, could be called a bold new approach to starting Alliance churches. It won't work everywhere. And even here we have been reminded that no ministry grows without pain, delays and trouble. This definitely is a "good news / bad news" story.

First, some good news. Phase I of our master site plan is now open on the church's 7.25-acre campus on Rita Road. Mortgage payments will come from income generated by Noah's Ark Day Care Center.

Phase II will feature a seventy-unit retirement center—The Willows at Rita Ranch. There will also be a fellowship hall and a fully-developed location for Noah's Ark Day Care Center. Mortgage payments for Phase II will come from the income of The Willows.

How Did All This Come About?

The Alliance at one time had three churches

in Tucson. Two of them, First Alliance and Wilmot Neighborhood, were in trouble, and by late 1994, both were officially closed. Some people from each congregation began to meet together under the interim leadership of Pastor Charles Dale. It gave each group opportunity to get acquainted—and to think about the day when they would move eight miles south to Rita Ranch.

Rev. Bill J. Vaughn, superintendent of the Alliance's South Pacific District, deserves a lot of credit for what has been accomplished. Superintendent Vaughn is an entrepreneur. He thinks big.

"[The Alliance] has been really good at starting small churches," Mr. Vaughn often comments. "We've hit what we've aimed at. Let's raise our sights!"

When Vaughn saw the situation in south Tucson, he aimed for the stars! Rita Ranch was an eight-square-mile residential development projecting ultimately 20,000 residents. At the time there was no church in the area! And real estate was white hot.

With collaboration from the Alliance Development Fund, Vaughn purchased thirty-six acres along Rita Ranch Road at $10,000 an acre. A year later, in 1995, he sold thirty acres at $12,833 an acre. Rita Ranch Community Church had six prime acres debt free!

A Reluctant Player

When Rev. Bill Vaughn contacted me about going to Rita Road, I said no. Things were going very well for me at Fairhaven Church in Dayton, Ohio. We had a large ministry staff. My wife, Lynetta, and I were not interested in a move to Arizona. Three times Mr. Vaughn asked us. Three times we said no.

Not one to give up easily, Vaughn asked, "How can you say no if you haven't at least looked?" It was a fair question. Lynetta and I agreed to have a look.

Unquestionably, Rita Ranch was impressive. But I really did not aspire to plant a new church. I knew it probably would mean serving "solo" again after the luxury of fellow staff members. And although money isn't every-thing, I wasn't enthusiastic about a significant cut in pay. But the "Star Trek" mentality be-hind all of this was inspiring! We said yes.

Although the decision to return West was born out of faith, it was not an easy adjust-ment. Friends and family questioned the wis-dom of this move. Sometimes Lynetta and I questioned our own sanity!

Building the Team

Once it was settled that we would go, I asked David York, pastor of Wilmot Neighborhood, if he would serve with me. I also invited Ben

Findley, former worship leader at First Alliance. Both men agreed!

March 1, 1995, was my first day on the job. I called together members of the core group who knew how to pray. I asked them to be an Intercessors Team for Rita Ranch Community Church. This whole venture would never get off the ground without God's active hand in it.

With three couples on our ministry team, we were doing better than I had imagined. But God had another pleasant surprise. Later in March I received a call from my son-in-law, Matt Coleman, at Simpson College. He needed to do an internship for the summer. Could we work something out at Rita Ranch? We surely could! Matt and Susan joined the staff team, now eight strong—when I feared I would be doing it all alone! Matt and Susan served not just for the summer but voluntarily for a whole year. (Now they've returned to fulfill their required pre-appointment home service as accredited missionary candidates with the Alliance.)

God Provides Another Miracle

Rita Ranch Community Church had property. It had a pastoral staff. It had a loyal core of people, many of them members of the Intercessors Team. We did *not* yet have a building on our property. And therein lies the story of another miracle.

I had been in Tucson only a few weeks when

God arranged a meeting between the superintendent of schools, Calvin Baker, and me. It was not one of those hat-in-hand appointments. I had not gone to see him specifically to ask for a meeting place. But when he learned that I was the new pastor of Rita Ranch Community Church, he asked where the church would be meeting.

"We're still searching for a place," I admitted.

"Desert Willow Elementary is out there," the superintendent said. "It will be opening in late August. It's available."

With a temporary meeting place, prayer backing and a ministry staff, we were off to a good start. And we had the financial equity of six acres of land. But clearly a permanent home of the size we envisioned required more financial equity than what we had in those six acres of property.

With First Alliance and Wilmot Neighborhood closed, both properties were put on the market. Wilmot sold almost immediately for $300,000. First Alliance didn't budge. Finally Siloam Freewill Church offered to rent the building. That story also has an unexpected twist. Ultimately Siloam purchased the property for $200,000—and became a Christian and Missionary Alliance church!

From the beginning, the six acres troubled me. Most churches would be glad for six acres. But we had big plans. I tried to get Superintendent Vaughn to let us have ten, but the numbers just would not work. Through negotiations with the owner of adjoining property we were able to get another 1.25 acres.

We thought we had a builder, but the arrangement fell through. Days later God brought me in contact with Steve Wilson, president of Tyger Construction. He made a visit to Rita Ranch and agreed to design and build Phase I of our master plan at cost! As I indicated, we are now occupying Phase I and Phase II is in progress.

More Than a Building

But the church is not the building. It is a community of people with a common purpose. Our purpose statement, hammered out in the first months of my Rita Ranch ministry, can be summarized this way:

> The purpose of Rita Ranch Community Church is to please and honor God (1) by fulfilling Jesus Christ's great commandments to love God totally and love our neighbors as ourselves (Matthew 22:37, 39) and (2) by fulfilling His great commission to make disciples of all nations by baptizing them and teaching them (Matthew 28:19-20).
>
> This will be accomplished by
> • worshiping God
> • developing caring relationships

- demonstrating and verbalizing the gospel
- sending workers into the four spheres outlined by Acts 1:8
- helping Christians mature in Christ

This process will result in a growing, spiritually healthy body of believers who, by demonstrating love to God, one another and the world in an atmosphere of prayer, speed the return of Jesus Christ (Matthew 24:14).

The "Pain, Delays and Trouble"

I've made it sound very straightforward, very simple. It was neither. Our architectural firm's design for Phase I came back from bidding $500,000 over budget. Our financial planner threatened a lawsuit. As with virtually every rented or leased facility, we had conflicts with the elementary school whose building we were using.

Nearly every step from land acquisition to completed structure involved unexpected and long delays. Perhaps hardest to take was that some of the people who promised to be part of Rita Ranch Community Church walked out the back door as fast as new people came in the front door. In the second year of operation, a serious conflict raised its ugly head. Only with sweat, tears and a lot of praying did the church come through that battle.

Today Rita Ranch is a diverse body of people.

Three races are represented on the Governing Board, which ranges from thirty-year-olds to sixty-five-year-olds. They work together extremely well. They provide leadership to a growing congregation of gifted, dedicated people.

Now completely off district subsidy, Rita Ranch is poised to plant a series of daughter churches. The staff and governing board continue to think like entrepreneurs. They want to boldly go to other places where the church has not yet been.

And, if it must be, they are prepared to take some flak along the way!

Voices from the Past

Syracuse, New York, Church Tests the Divide-to-Multiply Formula

Can a church multiply by dividing? Members of the Syracuse Alliance Church will answer with an unequivocal yes! For a number of years the large (424—average Sunday morning attendance) Syracuse church had thought about and dreamed about a daughter church. Last year the congregation put feet to their prayers. They gave eighty-four of their members and their assistant pastor to begin a new Alliance church in Lafayette.

They also gave a cash gift of $21,488 for down payment on four-and-a-half acres of property, including a large house that could be converted into a meeting place.

And what about the statistics? Three months after losing 85 of its members and adherents, the Syracuse church was averaging almost 400 in Sunday morning attendance. The Lafayette church had increased to 110, for a combined total sixteen percent higher than what the Syracuse church had been before the "birth." Missionary giving, which had jumped a spectacular thirty-four percent the year before, stayed essentially steady despite the large contribution toward Lafayette property.

Says Rev. Edwin E. Henning, pastor of the Syracuse Alliance Church, "The mother church and the daughter church have prospered in terms of new life begotten. We believe our Father will be glorified in years to come as more fruit is gathered."

—Rev. Gordon F. Meier, D.Min., *The Alliance Witness*, April 13, 1983

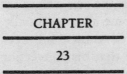

In Church Planting, Size Isn't Essential

by Steve Kiesel

S herwood Community Church in Council Bluffs, Iowa is proof that church *size* isn't the controlling factor in church planting. Rather, church *health* is. I can speak from experience. I am the pastor of Harvest Alliance Church, daughter church of Sherwood Community. Harvest Alliance is located in Minden, Iowa, a small community in southwest Iowa twenty-five miles from Council Bluffs.

You could say our church-planting venture took place in three stages.

Stage One

First, God stirred the heart of Steve Richert, pastor of Sherwood Community Church, to pray about an extension ministry in this general vicinity. Pastor Richert knew from preliminary studies that there was no evangelical, Bible-teaching, Christ-centered church in this area.

Having a heart for the lost, Pastor Richert specifically prayed for a "Lazarus." He wanted someone dead in transgressions and sins to see his need of a Savior and come alive spiritually. He wanted a person so well-known and even popular in the community that his conversion would impress a large number of people.

Pastor Richert began praying in 1989. In November 1992, God answered his prayer. A man in the area put his faith in Christ Jesus. The change in his life was apparent to his many friends and acquaintances. The first seeds had been planted.

Stage Two

Next, God began to prepare a group of people for the church planting. Actually, they were members of Sherwood Community Church living in the vicinity of Minden. They liked the Council Bluffs church. They had been attending it for some time. But driving to a church twenty-five to thirty miles away gave them little opportunity to impact neighbors and friends for Christ.

So they began a Sunday night Bible study in the Minden area. And they started praying about starting a church. They asked God to supply them with a pastor. That was stage two. The seeds were being watered.

Stage Three

Finally, God tapped me. I was born and raised in Shelby, a town seven miles east of Minden. In 1983, at the age of twenty-seven, I had become a Christian. As I learned more and more about Christ Jesus and what He had done for me, I matured spiritually. For some ten years I had been active in lay ministry at Sherwood Community Church. In August 1994, I applied to become a licensed minister of The Christian and Missionary Alliance.

When Pastor Richert presented to the Mid-America District his plan to begin a church in Minden, the final piece fell into place. The district gave me the opportunity to be pastor of this new work!

The church planting became official when, on March 12, 1995, Harvest Alliance Church held its first service at a rented facility in Minden. About forty people were present.

Both Churches Have Prospered

At the time Sherwood Community was contemplating a new church in Minden, Sunday morning worship was running just under 150. That hardly qualifies it for megachurch status. Yet God has enabled both churches to prosper and continue to bear fruit. After Harvest Alliance began, Sherwood Community's attendance dipped to a low of 98. But attendance soon rebounded to 139 and it has grown from there.

Others stepped in to fill ministry positions and do the work of those who had left. Despite the loss of some of the church's most faithful tithing families, finances never experienced any significant drop. Others must have increased their contributions to take up the slack. Best of all, Sherwood Community continues to lead people to Christ and make them a part of the church family.

In the short life of Harvest Alliance, God has also been active. As a result of the church's ministry at least fourteen people have trusted Jesus Christ as their Lord and Savior. We've seen some tremendous growth in the lives of individuals as they have applied God's Word. In April 1997, nine candidates followed the Lord in a baptismal service attended by ninety-five people.

Sunday morning attendance is now averaging sixty-two, and our meeting place has become too small. Our people are actively sharing their faith in Christ, impacting friends, neighbors and family. Last summer our church sponsored a Christian rock concert in a local park. Some 250 junior and senior high school youth attended and heard the good news about Jesus, our Savior and Lord.

God Gives the Increase

A couple of years ago, the Associated Press

reported a study done by an Iowa agricultural school. To produce 100 bushels of corn from one acre of land requires 4 million pounds of water, 6,800 pounds of oxygen, 5,200 pounds of carbon, 160 pounds of nitrogen, 125 pounds of potassium and 75 pounds of yellow sulfur. There are other elements as well, too numerous to list.

In addition, rain and sunshine at the right time are critical. The study estimated that only five percent of a farm's output can be attributed directly to the labor of the farmer.

The same is true in producing spiritual fruit. Some plant, some water, "but God made it grow" (1 Corinthians 3:6). God selected a fruitful, healthy church (Sherwood Community) to establish another fruitful, healthy church (Harvest Alliance). Being rooted in Christ is the key to a healthy mother church, the key to a healthy daughter church. It is healthy churches—not necessarily megachurches—that God seeks for church planting.

No Alliance Church? Start One!

You have moved and cannot find a new church—there are simply too few conservative churches in your area. And most of them lack the missionary emphasis and evangelistic vision you miss from your church back home. What would happen if you tried to start an Alliance church in your new community? Would your district office be interested? Could you begin a church that would succeed?

Says Rev. Paul Radford, national director of extension, "Laymen are a key to opening new churches. Lay people also make key leaders once a church gets off the ground. If they are the church planters, they will stick with the effort through thick and thin. Sometimes an extension pastor becomes discouraged, but these people will stay on and keep the work going.

"We want to be a church-planting denomination. I look forward to the time when, if we do not start 200 new churches, we will consider it a poor year. One key ingredient for this kind of effort involves our laymen; when they move to a new area that needs an Alliance church, they should phone their district office and ask how they can help start a church. I have heard of scores of cities where this has happened already."

—Warren Bird,
The Alliance Witness,
October 9, 1985

The Master's Master Plan

by Douglas L. Grogan

It was March 1994. I was the new director of church planting for the western sector of the Alliance's sprawling MidAmerica District. My phone rang.

"I'm Bill Janas from Del Norte, Colorado," said the voice on the other end. "I'm an English teacher and basketball coach at Del Norte Middle School. We have fifteen to twenty people meeting in our living room for Sunday worship and Bible study. Can we become an Alliance church?"

I about fell off my chair. You plant churches by commissioning a young pastor and his family to go to a targeted community. He struggles and prays much to assemble a core group of interested people. Here was Bill Janas in Del Norte, Colorado, who had done all the legwork for us!

I set a date the next month to meet Bill in Del Norte.

The Story behind the Story

Bill Janas was born and raised in Del Norte, a community in south-central Colorado. It is nestled in the foothills of the Rio Grande National Forest. The famous river forms the town's northern border. Together with several other towns, the area has well over 15,000 people to be reached with the gospel.

Bill attended and graduated from Adams State College in Alamosa, Colorado, where he met his lovely wife, Derissa. He hoped for a teaching job in Del Norte, but while he waited for an opening, he took a post in Colorado Springs.

Looking for a place to go to church in the Springs, Bill and his wife happened on the Alliance's newly planted Cheyenne Mountain Fellowship. Cheyenne Mountain Fellowship had been the vision of Rev. Daryl Dale, then the Alliance's director for Christian Education. Daryl felt the need for an Alliance church in that area of Colorado Springs. He began going door to door, sharing his vision with neighbors. In a short time he had some sixty interested people.

Bill and his family liked Cheyenne. They liked the clear way the Bible was taught. They enjoyed the contemporary worship format. They appreciated the church's concern for young people. But it wasn't too long until Bill received his opportunity to move home to Del Norte. And the impact of Cheyenne Mountain Fellowship stayed with him.

In Del Norte Bill and his family looked for a church like Cheyenne. None. They desired a church with contemporary worship, a strong emphasis on the Scriptures and a vision for community youth.

As Bill shared this vision in a quiet way, he found others who were looking for the same thing. Little by little there was a drawing together of interested people: fellow teachers, students, parents. Cheyenne Mountain Fellowship, itself yet young, was unknowingly giving birth to a church 250 miles away! Life begets life.

I Visit Del Norte

I cannot forget that April afternoon when my wife and I arrived in Del Norte for our visit. The view of the sun-bathed mountains with their evergreens and snow-capped peaks was awesome. Over grilled steaks and baked potatoes, Bill and some of his associates shared enthusiastically with us their church vision. They had even chosen a name: Cornerstone Community Church of The Christian and Missionary Alliance! And they had developed a brochure sharing their vision statement with the community. This group was primed to go!

Before the evening was over, we had agreed that finding a pastor was the next step. But he must be someone who would fit both the vision and the area. We all agreed to make this need a matter of prayer.

I didn't have to wait long for God to show me His man. The very next afternoon I had an engagement at Aurora Alliance Church in Denver. Pastor Don Brust had arranged for me to meet with a young couple who were assisting Aurora in a church-planting project.

Vance and Colleen Grace were students at Denver Theological Seminary. Both were graduates of Crown College. Vance had another year of seminary before finishing.

Vance had been raised in Wyoming. He loved to hunt and fish. He and Colleen desired a location in the West, preferably in or near the mountains. A small town was fine, as long as it served a wide enough area. As I talked with Vance and Colleen, I sensed we had our couple for Del Norte!

Delayed Action

When Vance and Colleen met with the group in Del Norte, both sides were impressed. But neither Vance nor Colleen was prepared to forfeit Vance's final year at the seminary. And the Del Norte people had hoped for someone a bit older. Vance returned to seminary and the Del Norte group heard other candidates.

At the time of the district conference that fall, Vance, who was present, took me aside.

"Regarding Del Norte," he said, "I am open to an invitation if this is what God wants." We continued to pray. And soon I had a call from Bill Janas in Del Norte.

"Could Vance and Colleen come back for another visit?" he wanted to know. I phoned Vance and the trip was arranged. In December 1994, Vance became the first pastor of Cornerstone Community Church in Del Norte. Over the next six months he traveled once a week to Denver to complete his seminary work, graduating in May 1995.

A Building and a Piano

Del Norte had its pastor. But there was still the matter of a meeting place larger than Bill Janas' living room. In Del Norte, meeting places were few and far between. Soon after Vance and Colleen's arrival, Ken Bailey offered a solution. Ken Bailey was principal of Del Norte Middle School and, from the beginning, an enthusiastic member of the church's core group. He also owned a local restaurant, Stone Quarry Pizza. The historic, 100-year-old building housing the restaurant was constructed of locally quarried stone. Situated in the middle of town, it had a second story hall capable of seating 100. Bailey offered the second story at a very nominal monthly rent.

The church hung a large new sign on the front of the building, and the upstairs hall became the church's first home. Access to the room was up a flight of discouragingly narrow stairs, but the church continued to grow. So did the worship team. The Lord gave them a pianist, a couple more guitarists and singers.

Community people were attracted to both the worship and the Word.

Along with the pianist, God gave them a used piano. But as the truck bearing the piano rounded the final corner, a strange thing happened. The piano fell out, tumbling end-over-end, breaking into a thousand pieces along Del Norte's main street. Some people are sure God was mercifully sparing the movers from trying to get that heavy piano up the narrow flight of stairs!

Whatever the reason, God still provided. Someone gave the church a nearly new, lightweight Yamaha Clavinova.

Property and a Building

Earlier the church had looked at eighteen acres of land four miles west of Del Norte. On it was an 8,000-square-foot medical complex. The location was ideal, but the $160,000 price was steep for a beginning church.

Knowing they would soon need to find some place other than the upstairs hall, the church took another look. It offered the owners $130,000. There was some dickering, but for $130,000 the church ended up with fourteen acres of commercially zoned property and the large building. The district was able to grant Del Norte $30,000 outright. A loan from the Alliance Development Fund covered the balance. God provided in a big way!

Cornerstone Community Church was organized in the summer of 1996 with more than forty charter members. In October 1996, it dedicated its newly renovated building.

Cornerstone is impacting Del Norte and the whole region. People are turning to Christ. Lives, homes, marriages are being restored. Cornerstone already has established itself as the dominant church in the area.

And it is looking at Pagosa Springs and Durango. Cornerstone members want to develop a second worship team that can assist in planting churches in those communities.

May God cause their tribe to increase!

Conclusion

Easter 100 . . . An Unfinished Story!

Beginning the Monday following Easter Sunday, calls began coming into my office from the United States, Canada and Australia. The inquiry was always the same, "We have been praying and want to find out what happened on Easter Sunday."

Hundreds of churches prayed regularly in prayer meetings and worship services for the effort. Hundreds of Alliance people helped hand-address envelopes containing letters to be sent into target communities. God is honored by this evangelistic unity and has given us a harvest of persons won to Christ, and that harvest is still going on as you read this article.

On Easter Sunday, April 19, 1987, more than 10,500 people—most of them newcomers to The Christian and Missionary Alliance—attended the new Easter 100 extension churches and other established churches that used the Easter 100 evangelism strategy. Best of all, hundreds of new names from all over the United States and Puerto Rico were recorded as receiving Christ.

Our faithful Lord provided 101 Easter 100 churches that averaged 88 in attendance. The smallest attendance was in Blackfoot, Idaho, with 21 persons present on Easter Sunday. The largest was in Keizer, Oregon, with 302 people.

Both had successful beginnings. In Blackfoot, where two church-planting denominations had given up and left town, 27 persons showed up on the second Sunday, a return of over 100 percent. In Keizer, 190 people returned for the second Sunday. Best of all, both churches reported conversions and other spiritual victories.

More than 300 conversions were reported in Easter 100 churches on the first Sunday, and a steady stream of reports are coming in of more conversions as careful follow-up has taken place. Reports of decisions made by a Jehovah Witness in Connecticut, a cultist in Oregon and Roman Catholics in New York confirm the truth of the Scripture, "The harvest is plentiful . . . " (Matthew 9:37). Most of the churches that carefully followed the strategy reached a high percentage of unchurched people—many higher than 80 percent.

As we rejoice in God's abundant goodness, let us continue to pray much for Easter 100 pastors. Some of them are discouraged because their attendance did not meet their expectations. Others are finding church planting more difficult than they imagined. Satan, of course, is trying his best to defeat churches who target the unsaved.

When you pray, ask God to confirm His Word in the hearts of every Easter 100 pastor and ministry team. "Now to him who is able to do immeasurably more than all we ask or imagine . . ." (Ephesians 3:20-21).

—Paul Radford,
The Alliance Life,
June 24, 1987

<table>
<tr><td>CHAPTER
25</td><td></td></tr>
</table>

Run to the Darkness!

We live in a day when the American culture has been increasingly secularized. There are more unsaved and unchurched people residing in the United States today than ever in its history—over 195 million souls. During the last ten years, the combined membership of all Protestant denominations has declined by 9.5 percent (4,498,242) while the national population has increased by 11.4 percent (24,153,000).[1] In 1996, half of all churches in America did not add one new member through "conversion growth."[2] Church attendance is in rapid decline. Consider the following trend:

1991   49 percent said they attended church regularly.

1992   47 percent said they attended church regularly.

1993   45 percent said they attended church regularly.

1994	45 percent said they attended church regularly.
1995	45 percent said they attended church regularly.
1996	37 percent said they attended church regularly.

We're seeing the church lose whole segments of society. In all probability, North America is the only continent where Christianity is not growing.[3] Existing churches are not even keeping up with the population increase. Jim Montgomery emphasizes in *Then the End Will Come*:

> In not a single one of our 3,141 counties did church attendance increase at a rate faster than general population growth during the whole decade of the 1980's. We are barely winning enough of our children to the Lord plus an occasional outsider to keep the Church from actual decline.[4]

Furthermore, the numbers of churches available to keep the light of the gospel shining are declining. Montgomery continues:

> Our record makes a mockery of our theological beliefs. We no longer represent a powerful force either in our Jerusalem and Judea—among home grown Americans—in our Samaria—among all

those cultural groups that have migrated to our shores—nor yet in the uttermost parts of the earth among those still unreached peoples.[5]

Church consultant Tom Clegg has made the following observations:

> The United States of America, a supposedly Christian nation, leads the world in every category of violent and domestic crime and social decay. Further, the social indicators for those in the Church are the same as those outside the Church. *Therefore, what the Church is doing is having no effect on American behavior.*[6]

What was once the number one sending nation of foreign missionaries is now the thirteenth largest receptor nation. "We have become a society that fifty years ago, every denomination would have felt compelled to missionize."[7] For these reasons most have concluded that the U.S. is now *post-Christian.* We are living in the post-Christian age of American culture because the tide of culture, values and morals is moving decidedly away from Christianity. The established Church, with all of its resources, is apparently having little impact on our fast-failing civilization.

What Should We Do?

The late prophet/philosopher of the late twentieth century, Francis Schaeffer challenged us decades ago with this question: "How shall we then live?"

Every day we confront darkness all around us. It only takes a casual stroll down the street, a few minutes of watching the television or listening to talk radio. Maybe a discussion with a secular colleague or neighbor magnified the extent of the darkness to you.

As our American secular, amoral and agnostic philosophy of life increases, so will the despair index. With that will come a new openness to spiritual solutions. People cannot deal very long with a world devoid of hope. Yes, we are living in a day of much spiritual darkness, but also a day of great opportunity for those who know the power of the gospel and are willing to point the way to the Savior.

Several options are available to Alliance people and believers everywhere. We can lament the darkness, shut out the darkness, run from the darkness or *run to the darkness with the light of the gospel*. We have written to challenge this generation to opt for the last alternative. Every disciple of Jesus needs to become a disciple-maker. Each of us who believe in salvation by faith in Jesus Christ *alone* must live as if "there is no other name under heaven given to men by which we must be saved" (Acts 4:12).

Advocates for the Lost

We in The Christian and Missionary Alliance must become advocates for the lost who do not know who Jesus is or what He has done for them. We must unite in our resolve to make disciples in our town, the next town and the next unreached area of our region. We have written this volume to incite a new passion for church planting among our nearly 2,000 established churches in America. Our passion is not born out of a desire merely to reach for some new numerical goal, but to join those committed to evangelizing this nation. I join with Larry Lewis, President of the Southern Baptist Home Mission Board, when he states,

> Our real goal is to see to it that no human being could be born and live and die in these United States and territories who has not had the gospel clearly proclaimed to him, who has not had the opportunity to lay hold of the promises of salvation through Jesus Christ, who has not had opportunity to become part of a vital, Bible-witnessing, ministering congregation of people.[8]

Planting the Power

Every time a new church is planted, we plant the power of the gospel. Planting the power was the pattern of the early Church. Planting the power was the pattern of the early American Church. Planting the power was the pattern of the early Alliance Church. The stories we have told in this volume demonstrate that planting the power is the continuing passion of Alliance people.

I once heard Lee Rouson, former running back for the New York Giants, speak to a men's group I was a part of. He showed us one of his two Super Bowl rings and then told us why his New York Giants were able to beat out twenty-seven other teams for two years to achieve their goal. "I can sum up the secret in two words," he said. *"Unified effort!"*

The Giants during those two years achieved the elusive and rare combination of bringing together players who were absolutely committed to make an absolute effort. Every member of the team in those two years was unified in his desire to do whatever it took. He was willing to give 100 percent to make it happen.

Our "Super Bowl" equivalent is the successful evangelization of the United States. With unity of purpose and an all-out effort, we can plant the power in every county, every town, every unreached people group.

The challenge before us is to honor those who have gone before us and do all in our power to finish the job they so nobly began. If we will, we can. If we can, we must! Our Lord invites us to join Him as He leads the way. Perhaps some day soon we will join the Methodists of old in singing,

> The infidels a motley band
> in counsel met and said,
> "The churches are dying across the land,
> and soon they'll all be dead."
> When suddenly a message came
> and caught them with dismay:
> "All hail the power of Jesus' Name.
> We're building two a day!"

Join me in determining to run to the darkness with the message of hope that is the gospel of Jesus Christ. Let us make disciples and plant churches all over the place and bring back the King!

> *Let this gospel of the kingdom be preached across the United States and around the world, in every town as a testimony to every community of people. Let these churches reproduce themselves by raising up workers for the harvest from the harvest and sending out the called ones. Let this gospel become known among every tribe and people—and then the end will come. (Matthew 24:14, paraphrased)*

Notes

[1] Charles Arn, Autumn '96 American Society for Church Growth, *Journal of Church Growth*.

[2] American Society for Church Growth statistics.

[3] Statistics gleaned from George Barna, *Church in the World Today*.

[4] Jim Montgomery, *Then the End Will Come* (Colorado Springs, CO: Dawn Ministries, 1997), p. 144.

[5] Ibid.

[6] Clegg is Executive Director of Church Development and Extension with Open Bible Standard Churches. Recorded from a report given during a Church Resource Ministries seminar.

[7] Ibid.

[8] Ibid, p. 147.

An Open Invitation

The Christian and Missionary Alliance is looking for men and women:
- who have a pioneering spirit
- who have a passion for evangelizing the lost
- who are willing to be trained to successfully plant evangelistic and reproducing churches.

If you are such a person, I urge you to contact your district office or the National Church Planting Ministries Office. I'd love to talk to you! May the Lord bless you as you continue to seek your place of service in His kingdom.

The Christian and Missionary Alliance
Church Planting Ministries Office
620 Bonnymead Avenue
Harrisburg, PA 17111
(717) 558-5952
McNoel@juno.com

Appendix

Where Do We Go from Here?

Undoubtedly, the high watermark for The Christian and Missionary Alliance in the U.S. and its efforts to plant new churches came in 1987, when over 100 churches were planted on Easter Sunday, and a total of 148 were planted that year. That was followed by the heroic effort to reach a faith goal of planting 1,000 more Alliance churches by 1994.

According to Dr. Robert Logan, church-planting expert, "the leadership demonstrated by the C&MA during these days stimulated many denominations to reexamine their commitment to church planting." Not only were 594 churches added to the denomination during this effort, but the Alliance became a leader in the field of church planting. Dr. C. Peter Wagner was so impressed by the effort that he commended it in his book *Church Planting for a Greater Harvest* (Regal, 1990, pp. 16, 106-107).

One is sobered by the prospect of an Alliance without these churches today. They have added to the diversity of our movement; they have taken the rich message of the Christ-centered Fourfold Gospel to new venues; they have contributed to the fulfillment of the Great Commission through intentional outreach in their communities and support of our worldwide mission by giving to the Great Commission Fund. The Alliance tapestry is indeed enriched by the inspired effort of those days.

Some Objections Have Been Raised

Interestingly enough, some have been very critical of the emphasis of these days. The criticisms fall into two main categories. The first suggests that the effort was a top-down national office-driven initiative. Those who hold this view argue that there was much pressure to perform [plant] placed on districts and through them upon churches. It is alleged that "getting the numbers" became the driving value above all else.

Reflections

In response, two observations can be made. First, the "double in a decade" effort was endorsed if not initiated by Council action. This convocation brings together representatives from the churches of the Alliance. It could be argued that this faith venture was birthed at the grassroots level. Certainly those people representing the churches adopted the idea. Second, the material produced during this era to assist the churches in church planting was principle-driven, not numbers-oriented. The call was to make disciples and extend the kingdom. It was an early admonition to "win-build-equip-multi-ply-send!" One is hard-pressed to find any emphasis on numbers other than asking every church to do "something" to support our jointly owned vision. The core value of this movement was that Alliance churches ought to be reproducing churches, a virtue much in evidence in the New Testament Church.

A Second Objection

The second objection to the emphasis of these days has to do with the observation that there were many "casualties," planters who were not successful in completing the planting task they set out to do. Some who attempted to plant were not well suited to the task they were given. Most were not adequately prepared for what they encountered. Support networks for those in the field were not complete. For many planters there was a sense of overwhelming task coupled with abject isolation. Yes, there were some who were hurt by the experience. Many have been forced to re-examine their call to ministry, particularly pastoral ministry.

Reflections

Most Alliance churches were not prepared to birth a new congregation. Some had never even considered this as a local ministry, thinking that "the denomination" was responsible for new church plants. Add to this those who ventured out from established churches and became disillusioned by the "way the new church turned out" when it did not quite match up with prior assumptions and expectations.

Another factor that has contributed to a negative impression for some is the way that districts arrived at their goals for church planting. At best, a district committee assigned a goal to the district churches. At worst, a single individual envisioned a goal and assigned it to the district churches.

The salient point is that the churches were not really integrally involved in this critical phase of the effort. As a result, many districts set goals that were beyond any reasonable expectation of fulfillment, even with room for much faith. When a given district did not come close to reaching its public goals, it became a negative experience for district churches.

These are only a few of the issues that have contributed to the reaction on the part of some to this period of time. Mistakes were made in the communication and vision casting of the faith venture. There was not an adequate church-planting infrastructure in place among the districts to sustain the movement. Some churches were frustrated by being asked to do something they were not reasonably equipped to carry out. Indeed, not every attempted church plant was successful.

Issues for the Future

Church planting is arguably the most difficult ministry task in the kingdom. The demands upon the individual church planter to bring something out of nothing are enormous. The task is complex and a "church-planting" pastoral training track until recently has not been available in most colleges and seminaries. Church-planting specialists have identified nineteen skill sets that need to be applied to the church planting context. Each plays a vital part in the success of the planter. They are:

1. Visionizing
2. Focusing
3. Planning
4. Listening
5. Praying
6. Evangelizing
7. Worshiping
8. Discipling
9. Mobilizing
10. Coaching
11. Leading
12. Unifying
13. Multiplying Ministry
14. Leading a Cell Group
15. Coaching Cell Leaders
16. Starting/Reproducing Cells
17. Personal Organization
18. Personal Integrity
19. Personal Spirituality

These skills are in addition to the training needed for orientation to the Alliance and its policies and distinctives.

It should also be noted that the training materials that are available for church planters have been largely developed since 1990. This is true both inside and outside the Alliance. When we reflect back on the seeming shortcomings of ministers during a specific period of time, it is wise to consider the circumstances of the day and their attendant limitations.

Today church planters know much more than we knew then. We have the advantage of building upon the costly foundations that others have laid. In the areas of prayer mobilization, spiritual warfare, planter assessment and coaching systems we have made enormous strides. We have good reason to believe that we are better positioned today to join the modern movement of God that is the multiplication of new churches.

Dr. Charles Arn has stated that since 1990 American Christianity has annually closed approximately 4,000 churches while opening only around 1,100. The Alliance has done considerably better than this, showing a net gain in churches each year. Since 1993 the Alliance has settled into a range of sixty-five to seventy-five new church plants per year. This indicates a planting rate of three to four percent of existing churches. However, the differential between churches opened and those closed was reduced to one percent in 1996. Unfortunately, 1997 records indicate the smallest number of churches planted since 1973. This was accompanied by a normal closure rate resulting in a small net loss in total Alliance churches. As we church planters continue to address the health needs of existing churches, we dare not neglect the reproducing of healthy Great Commission churches.

A New Day and a New Plan

The Christian and Missionary Alliance stands before an open door of opportunity. As many churches close inside and outside the Alliance, what will become of the communities formerly ministered to by them? As the cultural and ethnic diversity of the U.S. continues to increase, who will target these people groups and take the gospel to them in a relevant manner? What of the millions of urban Americans who have never been churched and are in need of the Savior? Will the Alliance reassert its essential nature as a church-planting movement? Will we put ourselves in a position to share in the harvest that our God is orchestrating? Will we join in what our Lord is doing as He builds His Church and extends His kingdom?

The challenge before the Alliance is to develop the infrastructure needed within our districts to sustain a church-planting movement. This will take the form of reproducible assessment, training and coaching/mentoring systems aimed at developing careful, intentional preparation for the planter and core group prior to launch. The infrastructure aims to give our districts the ability to plant churches that will plant churches. The goal is not a tree but a forest. The churches planted in this philosophy are convert-driven, not transfer-driven. "Winning, building and equipping" new disciples of Jesus Christ is the clear objective.

The area of the "healthy church" paradigm that is least developed in our districts is the "multiplying and sending" component. This training and coaching process will complement and complete the "Growing a Healthy Church" emphasis. It will give district leaders the tools and tracks needed to launch healthy Great Commission churches that will catalyze the fulfillment of our mission before Jesus returns.

Training Outcomes

The outcome of this training process will be the establishment of a comprehensive support system for church planters in every district. Furthermore, a plan will be in place to:
- find and carefully assess potential church planters;
- develop a comprehensive training track for every Alliance church planter;
- challenge healthy churches to reproduce themselves periodically and intentionally;
- support young churches in their early development;

- own a shared vision and value system that will supply the workers needed to fulfill our mission in the Alliance.

Four Faith Goals

With this process installed in our districts, the Alliance can envision the fulfillment of four faith goals. These are:

- A sustainable annual new church start rate of 7.5 percent of existing churches [in 1996 terms that would mean 147 new church starts in 1997]. The effect of this is to get us to a sustained level that matches our high watermark in 1987.
- A survival rate of 75-80 percent of church-planting projects. [The national evangelical average is 25 percent.]
- A sustained conversion growth rate in each plant of at least 25 percent. Thus every church planted should be able to double or daughter every four to five years.
- A shared value across the Alliance owned by district leaders, pastors and church governing boards that church planting is what we do, for the glory of God.

As these systems begin to emerge, the Alliance envisions a steady stream of new outlets for evangelizing America. These new churches will fully support and resource the Alliance as it pursues its global ministry vision into the next millennium. Perhaps the single most important issue facing the evangelical Church in general and the Alliance in particular is our commitment to planting reproducing churches. May the Lord grant us success as we pursue His lost sheep with the most effective evangelistic method known to man—church multiplication.

Participating Authors

Miss Linda Adams lives in Rome, New York. She is a member of Rome Alliance Church, where she is involved with worship and youth ministries. She works in the Northeastern District Office of Church Planting and Redevelopment.

Mrs. Jody Brown is a graduate of Nyack College. Jody, her husband, Jeff, and their three children have recently moved to Saline, Michigan. There Jeff serves as Director of Church Planting for the Alliance's Great Lakes District.

Rev. Jim Corley received his education from Simpson College and Western Evangelical Seminary, Portland, Oregon. In addition to leading Rita Ranch Community Church, he is a freelance writer. He and his wife, Lynetta, have four grown children.

Miss Neysa Costa, prior to her work as program director of Family Life Center, was an Alliance missionary to Burkina Faso, West Africa. She also serves on the Multicultural Ministries staff of the Alliance's Southern District.

Rev. Douglas L. Grogan has served since 1994 as Director of Church Planting for the Alliance Mid-America District. He and his wife, Peggy, live in Omaha, Nebraska.

Rev. F. Mike Grubbs, his wife, Carol, and their two children now live in Charlotte, North Carolina, where he is pastor of First Alliance Church. In addition to Grace Fellowship Chapel in Bedminster, New Jersey, Mr. Grubbs planted churches in

Cambridge and Coshocton, Ohio, while pastor of The Christian and Missionary Alliance Church in Zanesville.

Rev. John Keh-Jung Guu is associate pastor of Chinese Alliance Church, Fort Myers, Florida. He received his ministerial training at Ontario Theological Seminary, Toronto, and Trinity Evangelical Divinity School, Deerfield, Illinois.

Miss Patricia Heffernan is a 1987 graduate of Alliance Theological Seminary. Currently she serves with Alliance Jewish Ministries, assisting in church planting among Russian Jews in Brooklyn, New York. Pat spent two years ministering in the former Soviet Union with CoMission. She is under appointment as an Alliance missionary to Bosnia.

Pastor Steve Kiesel is a graduate of the University of Northern Iowa in Cedar Falls. Currently he is enrolled in the Alliance Ministerial Studies Program. He and his wife, Lynne, and their four children live in Shelby, Iowa.

Mrs. Edna Mapstone, her husband, Gerald, and their daughter Kristen live in Wheaton, Illinois. Gerald is superintendent of the Midwest District. Edna works part-time in the district office and is chairperson of the Midwest District Missions Committee.

Dr. Gordon F. Meier has served since 1990 as Director of Church Development for the Central District of The Christian and Missionary Alliance.

Dr. Michael D. Noel is the National Director for Church Planting for the U.S. Christian and Missionary Alliance. Prior to this, he served as the Director of Church Development in the Eastern Pennsylvania District of The Christian and Missionary Alliance.

Rev. George Reitz is the National Associate Director of Urban Church Planting for The Christian and Missionary Alliance. He and his wife, Judy, live in Astoria, New York.

Rev. Vergil Schmidt received his education at Criswell College and Criswell Graduate School, Dallas, Texas. Prior to his ministry in Midland, he pastored Alliance churches in Edmonton and Grande Prairie, Alberta, Canada.

Rev. Jefferson Taylor is a graduate of Toccoa Falls College and Dallas Theological Seminary. He has pastored Alliance churches in Spearfish, South Dakota; Arlington, Texas; and Reidsville, North Carolina.

Mrs. Linda Thomas lives in Greenfield Center, New York, with her husband and three children. Formerly a member of Pine Knolls Alliance Church, she is a founding member of New Life Fellowship.

Rev. David A. Toth has served the Ohio Valley District as Director of Church Planting since 1994. He and his wife, Marian, have four children.

Rev. David Wong grew up in Manila, Philippines. He holds a Doctor of Ministries degree from Trinity Evangelical Divinity School. Washington International Church is his third church-planting experience.